From
INQUIRY
to
ACTION

From
INQUIRY
to ACTION

Civic Engagement with **Project-Based Learning** in All Content Areas

STEVEN ZEMELMAN

HEINEMANN
Portsmouth, NH

Heinemann
361 Hanover Street
Portsmouth, NH 03801–3912
www.heinemann.com

Offices and agents throughout the world

Cataloging-in-Publication Data is on file with the Library of Congress.
ISBN: 978-0-325-06257-0

Editor: Tobey Antao
Production: Sonja S. Chapman
Typesetter: Kim Arney
Cover design and interior design: Suzanne Heiser
Manufacturing: Steve Bernier

Printed in the United States of America on acid-free paper
20 19 18 17 16   PPC   1 2 3 4 5

DEDICATION

To Susan, my wife and partner, who has fed me, laughed with me, and worked alongside me on her own invaluable teaching all through this project

And to the inspired teachers and energized students across this country who make inquiry and social action matter in their schools and communities

CONTENTS

ACKNOWLEDGMENTS

My inspiration for this work was ignited when two outstanding Chicago teachers, Elizabeth Robbins and Jean Klasovsky, gave speeches about their teaching and their students' learning for a TEDx event I organized in 2013. I was struck by Elizabeth's passion for students' active efforts to improve their communities and Jean's for Restorative Justice as a tool to create a supportive community in classrooms and across the school. I knew that something had been missing even in our best efforts to make learning meaningful and powerful for kids. All too often they are passive receivers of education instead of active and engaged participants. Elizabeth and Jean helped me almost instantly to realize what was missing and how we as teachers could help students step up and advocate for meaningful change themselves. You'll read Elizabeth's and Jean's classroom stories and learn about their thinking in the Introduction and Chapter 2 of this book.

I quickly learned that a great many teachers and researchers were courageously promoting similar kinds of inquiry that included social skill development, reading, writing, and responsible community action. A number of them generously shared their expertise and opened their classrooms and after-school clubs to me—Jen Cody, Lori McGarry, and Liz Cullin, the fifth grade team at Park Forest School in State College, Pennsylvania; Curriculum Coordinator Francesca Peck and math teacher Carrie Moy, at the Polaris Academy in Chicago; art teacher and Restorative Justice leader Mauricio Pineda at Reilly School, Chicago; Marnie Ware, biology teacher at Prosser High School, Chicago; Brad Latimer, math teacher at the Science Leadership Academy in Philadelphia, and Heather Van Benthuysen, English teacher at Alcott College Prep High School, Chicago. They and their students taught me in concrete detail how learning with civic action works and provided the stories and experience that are the heart of this book. The teachers shared the deep thinking, skillful action, and wise willingness to have students take the lead, that characterize the true educational expertise that so few outside of our profession are aware of.

The Mikva Challenge is the wonderful organization that promotes student voice and learning with social action in Chicago, and the Mikva educators and staff shared their knowledge and provided help and material at every step as I gathered ideas and stories for the book. I'm especially indebted to Jill Bass, Director of Curriculum and Teacher Development, Chris Rudd, facilitator of Mikva's city-wide students' Juvenile Justice Council, and Executive Director Brian Brady. Mikva's teaching guide, *Issues to Action*, will help any teacher make this work happen in his or her classroom. Mikva's influence is everywhere in this book.

The writings of a number of scholar/teachers across the country have provided thinking that especially helped me understand the wider importance and power of teaching and learning with social action—Meira Levinson, author of *No Citizen Left Behind*, Dana Mitra and Stephanie Serriere, authors of studies on student voice and activism, Brian Schultz, author of *Spectacular Things Happen Along the Way*, Kristina Berdan, *et al.*, authors of *Writing for a Change: Boosting Literacy and Learning Through Social Action*, Randy and Katherine Bomer, authors of *For a Better World: Reading and Writing for Social Action*, Celia Oyler, author of *Actions Speak Louder Than Words: Community Activism as Curriculum*, Smokey Daniels and Nancy Steineke, authors of *Teaching the Social Skills of Academic Interaction*, and Smokey Daniels and Sara Ahmed, who wrote *Upstanders: How to Engage Middle School Hearts and Minds with Inquiry*. Study these teacher-thinkers' works and you will understand how essential it is to bring teaching and learning with social action to the classroom, and how to make it happen.

Tobey Antao, my editor at Heinemann, brought her astute eyes to the manuscript, providing crucial suggestions that improved its organization, clarity, and impact. Managing Editor Lisa Fowler encouraged this effort from the start. Thanks, too, for the help from the rest of the Heinemann team—Sarah Fournier, Sonja Chapman, Suzanne Heiser, and Eric Chalek. I've treasured their enthusiasm for the project.

Finally, my thanks to all the many teachers and researchers across the country who I haven't met but who promote student voice and activism, or who seek to begin doing so by using this book—in spite of the social forces and policies that could easily discourage them. And to all the students who step up and accept the invitation to take initiative, and pitch right in to become active citizens who make a difference in their communities. Without you I'd be quite lost. This book comes alive only when your voices are heard.

—Steve Zemelman, Evanston IL, 2015

FOREWORD BY SONIA NIETO

One of John Dewey's fundamental ideas about education was that it should be about life, not just preparation for life (Dewey 1897). If this philosophy were followed, schools would be celebrating the efforts of teachers such as those featured in this book rather than only, as too often happens, demanding that they reach "adequate yearly progress" or that their students learn how to take tests. And if schools heeded a fundamental tenet of the philosophy of Paulo Freire (1970)—that education should be about *praxis,* that is, that intellectual work should be aligned with social action—then the examples in this book would be commonplace. But, alas, that is not yet the case.

Enter Steven Zemelman's *From Inquiry to Action,* with guiding principles, concrete strategies, and powerful examples that will help teachers and students dream up their own social action projects. Administrators too might rethink how they can support the teachers and students in their schools to become active community members. Who knows? Perhaps even some policymakers would take up the challenge to make this kind of education essential for all students. Then, we'd really have a sea change in U.S. education.

In these pages, Zemelman invites readers to look into schools to see what it means to bring classroom-based inquiry to community social action. From elementary through middle and high school, he highlights teachers who bring joy and commitment to their work with students. In turn, students learn that learning can be exciting, joyful, and relevant to their lives. Nowhere has it been more obvious that community social action can have tremendous benefits; it can even change how we think about education.

Students of all backgrounds benefit when schooling is relevant to their lives, but perhaps this is especially meaningful for young people who do not traditionally see their backgrounds and experiences reflected in the curriculum. For these young people, school is about *other people,* not about them or their families or their neighborhoods.

Consequently, they often feel adrift in school, a place where their realities are largely unacknowledged or even dismissed. But it does not have to be this way. Through social action projects grounded in their own communities and experiences, all students can develop not only academic skills but also a sense of purpose. There is no better antidote to dropping out of school than becoming motivated to continue their studies and, even more importantly, become active participants in their communities.

More than a recipe to follow, this book is brimming with inspiring stories about real students and teachers in real schools who decide to take risks and change, in small ways and large, situations that are unfair or wrong. As a result of engaging in these actions, in these pages the sense of empowerment they feel is palpable. Who would not want classrooms to vibrate with life and energy like the ones in this book?

There is little joy in schools these days: teachers feel blamed and disrespected, many students are disengaged, and the public is treated daily to pessimistic stories about the collapse of U.S. schools. At a time when hope for our nation's schools is in short supply, *From Inquiry to Action* is just the jolt of energy we need to restore our faith that schools can indeed be the incubators of active, caring, and committed citizens. Steven Zemelman deserves the gratitude of all of us who care about young people and the future of public education for bringing this beautiful book to fruition.

References

Dewey, J. 1897. My pedagogic creed. *School Journal*, 54, pp. 77–80.

Freire, P. 1970. *Pedagogy of the oppressed*. New York: Seabury Press.

~

INTRODUCTION

You've cracked open a book on linking powerful teaching and learning with students' social action, an approach that can transform education at many grade levels. It's filled with stories of great classroom instruction from grades five through twelve that include thoughtful student action in their communities. And it provides detailed how-to steps for teachers to guide similar efforts themselves. So what does this kind of teaching and learning look like? Let's not waste a moment but head to Elizabeth Robbins' history class at Hancock High School in Chicago to find out.

TEACHING, LEARNING, AND SOCIAL ACTION IN A HIGH SCHOOL HISTORY CLASS

As Elizabeth's juniors began the process of identifying the social action work they would tackle as a class, they spent several days surveying the assets in their heavily Hispanic Southwest-Side-of-Chicago working-class neighborhood. They listed churches and stores, interviewed neighbors to identify problems and issues, and searched the web (a useful website for Chicago would be "Dreamtown"—www.dreamtown.com /neighborhoods/chicago-neighborhoods.html—but other cities have their own sites documenting resources). Elizabeth also used news articles on neighbor-hood displacements over the years to get students thinking further about underlying issues that affected them. Then in small groups students brainstormed issues they considered most important in their lives and communities. This is a crucial moment, when students begin to realize they are going to be working on something that matters to them, and that the choice will be theirs. The seventh-period-history juniors narrowed their list to these concerns:

- High unemployment

- Racial discrimination

- Neighborhood violence

- Deportation of undocumented immigrants

- High cost of college attendance

- Juvenile justice

These were all huge issues, obviously, so to explore in any depth they'd need to focus more narrowly, once one was chosen. Students formed groups based on their interests, embarked on some initial research, and prepared presentations, complete with PowerPoint slides, to advocate for their chosen topic. They explained why their issue was important, who was affected, and what organizations were working on it. Students researching juvenile justice, for example, learned that teens were especially impacted by automatic waivers that switched trials for serious crimes from juvenile to adult courts. The class would be selecting just one issue, so once all the presentations had been heard, it was time to take a preliminary vote. Students in new small groups compared choices and reported the results:

- Use of waivers to try juveniles in adult courts: 16

- Neighborhood violence: 2

- Deportation: 2

The vote appeared overwhelming. But rather than go with the majority, Elizabeth asked the class a question that shows how strategic but measured guidance can make this kind of project truly transformative: "What will happen if we just accept the choice of the sixteen?" Students quickly observed that the losing four would tune out and disengage from the effort. Which led to Elizabeth's next question: "So how should we deal with the difference? How could we arrive at a consensus?"

"We should each give our reasons and hear from the others," kids responded. "We should discuss this." Again Elizabeth tossed it back to the students: "How should we do that?" The students chose a discussion strategy they'd already learned: four corners. They gathered in the corners of the room, based on their preferences (really just three corners, in this instance), to talk things over. As spokespersons for the groups began to report, however, the discussion devolved into a debate, so Elizabeth interjected: "Wait a minute. How is this going to get us to a consensus? You need to listen to one another."

After a few more back-and-forth rounds, several students proposed trying to look for common ground. This shifted the conversation, and speakers began groping for connections between the topics: deportations and trial waivers both create "bad vibes" in the community, they thought. Use of waivers to try juveniles as adults sends more kids to prison, where they learn to use more violence. They acknowledged the legitimacy of each other's choices. Elizabeth finally helped by observing that all three issues particularly affect minority communities. Even if the connections were a bit of a stretch, students were now listening to each other and appreciating various points of view. They'd experienced an important lesson in how to work together as a group and deal with honest differences. The class was now ready to begin researching the problem of prosecuting minors as adults, with a proviso to also include the effect of this policy on neighborhood violence, and the relationship of the policy to deportation of undocumented immigrants.

Fast-forward a week: students had discovered that a bill was under consideration in the Illinois State House of Representatives to end the automatic transfer from juvenile to adult courts. Now the kids were highly focused: How could they lobby legislators to pass the bill? And what was the process by which the bill would advance from committee to a vote on the House floor? Students who would have been deeply bored reading a textbook passage on American legislative procedure were eagerly trying to learn how the bill would be reviewed by the House rules committee. While one student called an assistant to Representative Barbara Flynn Currie, the rules committee chair, the others waited expectantly. But the news was grim: if the committee didn't vote before the impending end to the legislative session, the bill would die.

Alas, it's possible that too many legislators might have worried that they'd look "soft on crime" if they supported the bill, so the safest thing to do was to simply avoid voting on it. The students didn't accept defeat, however. They talked to Representative Elaine Nekritz, who sponsored the bill, and who in turn suggested they contact a Chicago organization called the Juvenile Justice Initiative. Its director visited the class and described the organization's ongoing campaign to get the law changed. The students decided on three actions to support the initiative's campaign to pass the bill the next year:

- A letter to the editors of the two major Chicago newspapers

- Web-based circulation of a petition

- A fund-raising campaign selling snacks (unhealthy, of course) to fellow students

Challenging Students to Make Their Own Decisions

Notice that this activity moved students beyond the kind of "argument" in the Common Core writing standards that focuses only on defending a position. Instead, they were exploring the more complex thinking needed to find deeper connections between equally important issues and to bring everyone on board.

Just as important to the learning process, Elizabeth rarely gave students explicit guidance, but she didn't remain silent either, instead repeatedly tossing questions and challenges back to them. In another class her students focused on the high cost of college, and hypothesized that an important factor could be the poor management of funds. But how would they research this? An observer in the classroom could barely control his desire to help, wanting mightily to suggest that they google a college's administration page to find a financial officer they could talk to. But fortunately he held back as Elizabeth masterfully pressed them: "What do you need to know? How can you find out about this?" When asked later about her insistence that they solve problems themselves, she smiled. "If I do this for them now, they'll never be able to do it on their own when they leave here."

Students reflected on her approach as well.

Marianna: Most teachers just tell us what to do.

Carlos: Since it's *our* topic, we should be the ones to decide how to work on it.

Marianna: She wants us to decide. But sometimes it's hard.

Alejandro: We're actually trying to *do* something.

Carolyn: We did projects for the history fair, but it wasn't as exciting.

And yet, there are times when the teacher *does* need to help and guide. More on this to come as you'll see teachers deciding throughout Chapters 1 through 4.

At the school year's end, the students were still at work. And their appraisal of their effort?

Carlos: *It's exciting to put a plan into action. I want to be able to make a change in the world.*

Marianna: *If we want to do something to improve our community, we'll know how to do it now.*

> To hear Elizabeth speak about teaching with social action, watch her TEDx talk, which inspired the writing of this book: www.youtube.com/watch?v=7 -lUrM-rmlE

LEARNING THAT MOVES FROM INQUIRY TO SOCIAL ACTION—A DEFINITION

As you can see in Elizabeth Robbins' students' project (she would quickly correct anyone who said it was just hers rather than the kids'), the work takes students through the process of choosing, researching, and actively working to influence a problematic policy in the community that is important to them. Students learn to be active and responsible leaders by actually seeking to promote change, rather than just being—*supposedly*—prepared to be leaders in the future. And as classroom stories will illustrate throughout the book, this can be done at almost any age, in almost any subject.

There are at least four major steps that students take in this process:

- Identifying issues important in their lives and community, and deciding on one to address

- Researching the chosen issue and deciding how to change or improve the situation

- Planning an action, including determining a goal for change; identifying who or what body in the community has power to make the change; and deciding how to approach that person or persons

- Carrying out the action

Two features are especially crucial to making the experience authentic and empowering for students. First, they must own the responsibility to make choices and decisions and to figure out solutions to problems themselves. The teacher of course facilitates the work, but leaves as much of the decision making as possible to the kids. Second, the work should culminate in some action focused on change in the school or community. It's not enough to just talk about change, or practice in mock legislatures. When students see adults actually listening to them with respect, *that* is when they begin to realize they have a voice and can make a difference in their world. Their efforts may not always succeed, but in being heard they come to value the studying, reading, writing, and planning that they have done. School and learning begin to truly matter.

WHY TEACH THIS WAY—AND WHY NOW?

Our kids can act silly and goofy, but when they interviewed and then presented their report to the town director of public works and the head of a local citizens' committee, they were so poised and mature. I was so proud of them, and I realized how important an authentic audience could be. And our school board heard about their impressive performance.

—Roosevelt Middle School teacher Laurie Hendrickson (in suburban River Forest, Illinois), after her Robotics Club students presented to officials their findings on the need for better flood protection for local homes

Why is it so important to conduct projects like this in our classrooms—at least some of the time—and why especially now? Well, first of all, school is our primary means of preparing children not just to be "college and career ready," but also "citizen-ready"— inviting them to be responsible citizens *now*, as Elizabeth Robbins declares, not just in the distant future. John Dewey told us that a key role of public education is to prepare citizens for participation in a democracy. But students need to experience the rush of being heard and acknowledged by adults in their community, or actually making something happen to improve it. It's the responses of people in the real world around them that teach young people how communities work and which words and actions can make a difference. In addition to caring and understanding, smart skills and strategies are needed to promote change, and students will learn them most effectively by actually trying them out and discovering what works.

Teaching with Social Action Provides Focus on Community

> When we teach government, we need to teach
> it in terms of relevance and access. But at its
> heart, it must have an action civics base.
>
> —Elizabeth Robbins, "Young People Are the NOW," TEDx talk

A second reason why this approach is so important is that American society's intense focus on individual achievement and well-being tends to eclipse *community* needs and efforts. Government agencies and public programs are viewed by many as ineffective, compared to the power of competitive private businesses. Yet many social needs cannot be met by private corporations that focus mainly on their own success—not because they are uncaring but because by definition that's not what they're designed to do. At the same time, many public institutions and policies don't always serve those social needs very effectively. They can be fraught with problems and imperfections that citizens need to address rather than simply dismissing them out of hand. Schools are some of the only public entities that can help strengthen the public commitment to community, since they can focus not just on an immediate result but on equipping the next generation to contribute. However, they aren't doing that as well as they could just yet. When Robbins asked, in her TEDx talk, how many audience members had taken a civics or government class, almost all two hundred raised a hand. But when she asked, "How many can say you learned how to be active members of your community in school?" just one lonely hand went up.

Teaching with Social Action Creates Stronger Student Engagement

> This isn't brain surgery. If you just open the door
> and give kids a chance to choose the issues they're
> passionate about, they will take on the toughest,
> most complex tasks, and they'll do all the work
> themselves, rather than leaving it to you.
>
> —Jill Bass, Director of Curriculum and Teacher Development at the
> Mikva Challenge organization in Chicago

Students who don't see the connections between what they are asked to learn and their own present needs often feel disempowered and bored in school. We know our subjects really matter and will help our kids understand and negotiate their world as they grow up—so why doesn't that yawning student in the third row get it? In fact, most young people are quite idealistic. They recoil at injustices and wonder why problems in their neighborhoods or the wider world don't get fixed. They long for peace and safety and mutual understanding. They want to experience agency and be actively engaged. They may claim not to care about school or what goes on around them, but that's usually just a pose to avoid their sense of powerlessness. Learning connected with action in the community grabs onto children's need to engage in meaningful, active, and empowering efforts.

Teaching with Social Action Improves Students' Mindsets about School

> The comments of Crown, a chronic truant prior to participating in this classroom [fifth grade in a school next to the Chicago "projects"], resonate strongly: "I did not feel school was a place for me. I didn't think it would help me in my life, but this project made me like coming to school . . . It did not feel like the boring school I was used to." His turnaround and newfound dedication to schoolwork and attendance demonstrated the power of a democratic classroom, where students were critical members encouraged to embrace their own ideas of what is worthwhile.
>
> —Brian Schultz, *Spectacular Things Happen*
> *Along the Way* (pp. 9–10)

Beyond just banishing boredom, connecting school with the world in which students live leads them to value learning and to feel a sense of belonging to the school community, resulting in higher achievement. Camille Farrington and her fellow researchers at the Chicago Consortium on School Research reviewed the studies on how student mindsets about school affect achievement. As they report in *Teaching Adolescents to Become Learners: The Role of Noncognitive Factors in Shaping School Performance* (2012), kids' attitudes make a major difference in their learning, and teachers can greatly influence these attitudes. Researchers and testing experts call such attitudes "noncognitive" factors—not because they don't involve thinking, but because they aren't measured by traditional standardized tests. These include positive mindsets such as:

- I belong in this academic community.

- My ability and competence grow with my effort.

- I can succeed at this schoolwork.

- This work has value for me.

Obviously, students who don't view learning in these ways are unlikely to work very hard on it. "If I'm not going to succeed anyway, why should I bother?" But one powerful way to strengthen these attitudes positively is to have students see how their learning can indeed make a difference in the real world.

An early practitioner of teaching and learning with social action, Brian Schultz (quoted above), in *Spectacular Things Happen Along the Way* (2008), tells how this approach altered attitudes as well as learning for his fifth-grade students in a Chicago public school in 2004. No doubt others conducted similar projects before this one, but perhaps they'll pardon the attention to this remarkable story. The students campaigned for a new school to replace their dilapidated building and achieved local and national fame. Ralph Nader visited during his presidential campaign and wrote on his website:

> *The youngsters appear transformed. Their attendance rate is 98 percent and coming from a part of Chicago rife with drugs, street violence, gang activity, physical deterioration and unemployment, this is testimony to their interest. They design each part of their research and action strategy. They learn how to do surveys, write different letters [to seek] support from politicians, community leaders and from their own peers. Nine hundred students from other schools have expressed their support.*
>
> —Ralph Nader, www.commondreams.org, April 20, 2004

Teaching with Social Action Gives Students Immediate Purpose for Learning Academic Skills

> The other thing I wanted to make sure you are aware of is how much your academic skills are being strengthened by the project. . . . When you look back on fifth grade I want to make sure you realize how much math and reading and writing and social studies you learned without even knowing it.
>
> —Columbia University Teachers College professor Celia Oyler, speaking to students while visiting Brian Schultz's classroom (in Schultz 2008, p. 108)

Children of course need to learn academic skills and content—math, history, science, literary analysis. As Oyler observes, applying learning to public action gives a purpose for these academic subjects, so they aren't approached as mere practice for some undefined future need that most young minds don't yet envision. Children live in the now. So when students know their arguments and proposals will be read with a skeptical eye next week by the city council or be published in the local newspaper, they become much more willing to revise, edit, correct their grammar, and, more broadly, to think about what reasoning will be effective with their audience. They'll be eager to research and find relevant information to bolster their claims. Teachers who engage students in working for solutions to community problems find that even attendance improves. Kids stop worrying so much about grades and instead focus on using their new skills to achieve real-world results.

Yes, But Can We Really Do This?

Especially nowadays, when there are so many skills to teach, so many mandates and requirements to address, tests to prep kids for, and curriculum to cover, is this kind of teaching and learning even possible in our classrooms? This is a question that thoughtful teachers and writers on student civic engagement ask themselves very seriously (Berdan et al. 2006, pp. 6–7, and Levinson 2012, pp. 257–288). After all, public school teachers are hired to serve the state and the public, and to teach curriculum mandated by the school board that hired them. Civic engagement projects can require precious time otherwise used to "cover" that curriculum. However, those mandates are made with a larger purpose—expressed in the mission statements of many schools and districts—to prepare the next generation to be productive and responsible citizens. Further, good teachers want students to meet and exceed standards in meaningful and engaging ways, rather than marching them through disconnected skill lessons that are promptly forgotten.

So here's the good news: this isn't an either-or situation.

The skills and content required by a state's adopted standards, even when these standards are imperfect, are inevitably addressed when students carry out the kinds of projects described here—though not necessarily in the order predicted by a traditional curriculum. Governmental mandates and social action in the classroom need not be mutually exclusive—as long as testing regimes aren't allowed to displace weeks and weeks of instructional time.

Teachers know, too, that children of all ages and backgrounds wish to improve the world around them, and that great teaching and learning can be built around that desire. These teachers seek tools to engage students in active roles in and beyond school, along with building traditional academic skills, because they see citizenship as more than a passive role. And they recognize the need to develop community consciousness among the future citizens sitting in front of them now. The urge to make the world a bit better than we found it remains a powerful motivation among America's teachers—one of the main reasons many chose this line of work in the first place—and it is a goal shared by many parents as well.

But this desire on teachers' part raises another question: With civic engagement in the classroom, can teachers keep from promoting their own political and social views with their students? (See Oyler 2012, pp. 5–6.) Certainly if the answer is no, the classroom would no longer be about educating children, but simply indoctrinating them. However, as you will see in the stories and strategies that follow, a central characteristic of this work is that the teacher, in fact, does *not* tell students what issues to tackle, what to believe, or what positions to take. Rather, he or she organizes activities so that students learn to make these decisions themselves, based on their own careful inquiry and reflection on conditions in their own lives.

So the answer is yes, teaching and learning with social action is not only possible, but urgently needed in today's schools. And good teachers are leading such projects in classrooms across the country.

Teaching with Social Action Provides Students with the Tools and Experience to Help Address Injustices in Their Communities

> There is a profound civic empowerment gap—as large and as disturbing as the reading and math achievement gaps that have received significant national attention in recent years—between ethnoracial minority, naturalized, and especially poor citizens, on the one hand, and White, native-born, and especially middle-class and wealthy citizens, on the other.
>
> —Meira Levinson, *No Citizen Left Behind* (pp. 32–33)

It's no secret—especially in light of recent and ongoing tragedies—that in spite of years of civil rights campaigning and some visible progress, poor and minority communities across the country continue to be denied many of the rights and resources they need to build productive lives and futures for their children. At the same time, too few members of these communities have developed the civic skills to obtain the opportunities they need. Sometimes they blame themselves or their neighbors, rather than coming to understand the structural forces that limit those opportunities. All citizens need the skills, knowledge, and sense of agency to find and seize these opportunities if we are to have healthy, democratic communities. By involving students in learning that leads to social action, teachers are promoting change right now as well as giving students the tools and mindsets to continue this work as they grow and mature.

In fact, *The Civic Mission of Schools* report by the Carnegie Corporation and the Center for Information and Research on Civic Learning and Engagement asserted in 2003 that addressing this need is a key task for schools—and the need is only greater today:

> *Civic education should help young people acquire and learn to use the skills, knowledge, and attitudes that will prepare them to be competent and responsible citizens throughout their lives. [This includes being able to] act politically by having the skills, knowledge, and commitment needed to accomplish public purposes . . . [and to] have moral and civic virtues such as concern for the rights and welfare of others, social responsibility, tolerance and respect, and belief in their capacity to make a difference. (p. 4)*

Happily, when a teacher like Adam Heenan in Chicago—another of the many educators using this approach—guides high school students through community action projects, the kids begin to leap across the gap and take on these civic roles. As one student in his class put it quite simply:

> *Before I didn't think I could actually make a difference, but now I am working with people at my church on antigang initiatives.*

Teaching with Social Action Is Invigorating and Meaningful for Teachers

I get the satisfaction of giving students the opportunity to carry out the kinds of efforts they'll need in order to be involved in their community. As a teacher, it's gratifying to see students work independently. It's exciting and makes me very proud. It reinforces my belief in the power of young people.

—Elizabeth Robbins, interview, June 4, 2014

Unlike the good old days (if those ever existed), teachers today often feel disempowered and blamed for the structural situations of their schools as well as society's larger ills. But connecting classroom and community offers an opportunity to show the world how our teaching really can matter. Helping students reach out into the community enables teachers to build relationships with outside community members and organizations, and in turn this lets those outsiders see the powerful learning taking place in our classrooms and the enthusiasm engendered in the students. Teachers are helping their students address some of those societal ills that do in fact make education more difficult. Taking action, even in small ways, goes far in dispelling the discouragement that teachers can experience when feeling passive and helpless.

How Is Teaching with Social Action Related to Project-Based or Expeditionary Learning?

Project-based and expeditionary instruction bear many similarities to the teaching and learning explored here, since they focus on real-world topics of importance, call for in-depth research, and invite students to create products for real audiences beyond just the teacher. But two major elements of teaching and learning with social action take students further and deeper:

1. **Student choice.** The focus of teaching and learning with social action is not just about student engagement, but about student *empowerment* as active citizens. This means that students learn to make their own thoughtful decisions by actively doing so now, during their education, rather than leaving educators to hope that, without any experience, this skill will magically develop later. By contrast, the project-based activities and units one usually sees in professional books, on websites, and in videos are mostly teacher-planned. They may be excellent, relevant, and engaging—but teachers are still the ones making the key decisions. Leaving so much to the students can feel risky. One can't know in advance just how the work will unfold. But, in fact, when students take the lead, they repeatedly surprise us with their intelligence, creativity, and tenacity.

2. **Action for improvement in the community.** Project-based learning usually leads to a product or outcome of some kind—a student-produced video, a PowerPoint presentation, a science demo—that embodies an issue or concept or topic students have learned about. They appreciate this and work hard to achieve strong results. The outcome in teaching and learning with social action, however, is specifically to seek some improvement in the community. This goes beyond traditional "service learning," such as volunteering at a food pantry, and includes at least an attempt to achieve some larger change. It may be a more modest

What About National Standards?

Many of us are not in love with everything in the latest standards—their internal flaws, lack of research support, links to problematic testing, and implication that every student should be learning the same things at the same time, while not getting much art, drama, storytelling, or anything else that many reformers mistakenly think aren't needed in the adult work world. The standards have nothing to say about making learning meaningful or connecting with students' lives and issues in their communities. True, the standards don't entirely reject these things, and in fact, the best professional writings and workshops on standards do aim to achieve them in meaningful ways. But we know that in too many school districts the focus will be on rote exercises and time-gobbling preparation for the tests that supposedly measure learning, rather than on those lively learning activities. In fact, one of the projects observed for this book was postponed because the school required every teacher to drop everything and focus on test prep—even though studies have found that such an approach doesn't help, and that *the best way to increase test scores is to focus on teaching our subjects* (Allensworth et al. 2008).

But right now, the standards are the order of the day for most of us. And the engaging research, analysis, argument, and speaking activities in this book actually address many of the most relevant Core standards, including writing for various audiences and purposes, researching in depth, reading critically, and building oral and collaborative skills. So the activity explanations provided in this book will, on occasion, take note of ways that standards are addressed. And many of us have seen that students who are engaged in studying and acting to achieve change in their communities also do just fine learning required skills, exceeding the standards, and performing on the tests. Nevertheless, we must keep in mind that the standards themselves tend to focus only inward, on practices like "close reading," which even if used thoughtfully do not help students learn how to participate responsibly in the wider world. Rather, the strategies used by teachers in this book are ones that will bring standards to life and make them worth pursuing.

effort to get a neighborhood park rehabbed. Or, as in one Chicago-area project, it may be something as important as guiding teens through the process of having nonviolent arrest records expunged from police files. It is this kind of attempt—and at least sometimes achievement—that leads young people to realize they can actively contribute to their community and needn't feel helpless about problems they see around them. Additionally, if we want students to transfer what they learn in our classrooms to their own lives, they need to experience and learn from the full process of social action, even (or especially) when that process is messy, recursive, or time-consuming.

Which Subjects and Grade Levels Are Right for This Approach?

You might think that civics and social studies classes are the natural homes for such learning, and of course they are. But teachers and students in any subject can productively engage in social action projects. English courses are especially appropriate when they focus on nonfiction reading, since so much material in that genre deals with large social, cultural, or environmental issues (though many plays and novels explore these areas as well). Science, particularly when it deals with environment or health, opens up many opportunities to connect with local and national real-world concerns. While many topics in math are more abstract, statistics and data analysis are key tools for much of the research that students will do when pursuing a social action project (see Chapter 4 for a great example of this).

For elementary teachers, of course, the question of subject relevance is much less an issue, since a single teacher may be responsible for every subject and can integrate a project with many elements of the curriculum without neglecting any of them. Wondering whether younger kids can do this? Chapter 1 tells the story of a group of three fifth-grade classes. Or check out the news article about a school in Montclair, New Jersey, where third-grade teachers guided students through the same kind of learning (Kaulessar 2015). Throughout the course of this book, you'll find examples and stories from every major subject area and a wide range of grade levels.

HOW THIS BOOK IS ORGANIZED

As you can see in Elizabeth Robbins' civic action project, students work through a series of steps to carry it out—steps that are transferable to any social action project. Chapters 1 through 4 take you through these steps with vignettes and practical strategies. In actual execution of a project, of course, the steps aren't necessarily confined to a particular order, and students may return to one or another step repeatedly as they pursue their goal. But they're presented separately to more easily explain how to support each aspect of the work. The ideas and strategies in this book are especially informed by the efforts of the Mikva Challenge, a Chicago organization that works with teachers and students on just such projects. Their curriculum guide, *Issues to Action*, follows a six-step process similar to that described here, and this book was extensively influenced by examples from teachers who work with Mikva.

So here's what you'll find in the chapters ahead.

- **Chapter 1: Choosing an Issue.** This can involve community surveys, reading text sets of short articles on current issues, hearing from visiting experts or officials from the community, holding discussions in small groups, or other activities. In many cases the whole class may work on a single issue, though as we'll see, it can also be effective for individuals or small groups to each tackle a concern of their own choice.

- **Chapter 2: Researching the Issue.** Now students go online, read more in-depth information, interview experts, gather data, organize their findings, inform one another about what they're learning, and explore a solution or solutions they wish to propose. Students will likely need plenty of support and guidance to find relevant, trustworthy material and they may need help with comprehending it effectively.

- **Chapter 3: Making a Plan and Preparing to Act.** This can take many forms, depending on the issue students have chosen. Usually, the work will involve determining key audiences to be reached—responsible officials, news media, governing boards, or community organizations. Students need to learn about various governmental agencies and organizations to understand whom they'll need to approach, and how officials in these organizations think. This will be followed by writing reports, proposals, letters to the editor, speeches, or other oral presentations. Support for students' writing is essential. Specific actions need to be planned out as well—fund-raisers, testimony to officials or boards, meetings or events to raise community awareness.

- **Chapter 4: Taking Action.** Again, activities and support will depend on the issue students have chosen, though there are suggestions for strategies to help the effort go well. More than ever, the teacher's role is to stand back as students carry out their planned activities. Reflection afterward is especially important. And teachers must think about how to help students deal with disappointment and value their effort whether they achieve their goal or not.

The remaining chapters of the book tackle the issues of building a foundation for this work in your classroom and taking this work beyond the classroom.

- **Chapter 5: Empowering Students in the Classroom.** If students are to engage in thoughtful public action based on their learning, we must shape classrooms to model and support it. Teachers should make their classrooms as democratic and participatory as possible, and this chapter explores three big elements of classroom process to help do this:

  1. Building classroom community so that students appreciate and support one another and have the skills and habits for working collaboratively.
  2. Organizing the classroom using a writing workshop structure to help students conduct the many stages of the work. While this chapter cannot address all aspects of writing instruction, it provides some essential strategies to adapt this highly effective framework for supporting almost any kind of student effort. A central part of a writing workshop is carefully defining the teacher's role—the teacher must be a model, but must also insist that students make as many of the decisions, choices, and problem-solving efforts as possible. The chapter explores this careful balancing act.
  3. Having crucial conversations as they arise. Whatever the topic at hand, students may express beliefs that raise issues of fairness, prejudice, human rights, or lack of understanding of others. It is essential for teachers to treasure these teachable moments and hold class discussions that examine such matters promptly, whether they fit in the required curriculum or not.

- **Chapter 6: Bringing Social Action to Relationships in the School with Restorative Justice.** This chapter moves beyond the classroom to look at a key way that teachers and students can make a difference across the school itself. Restorative justice involves a philosophy and a set of strategies that build community, prevent negative interactions, and repair harm caused when such interactions do occur. An increasing number of schools are adopting this approach to strengthen school culture using talking circles and peer juries or councils. It's especially relevant for learning with social action because it very effectively addresses the grievous issue of racial imbalance in the discipline practices in schools. So this chapter takes a look at how to initiate restorative justice practices. It describes the key strategies, including peer juries and peace circles, employed in one elementary school in Chicago. It then outlines steps and resources for establishing or strengthening such a program in your school.

- **Chapter 7: Growing an After-School Program.** There are many advantages to organizing teaching and learning with social action beyond the classroom. For teachers who want to work with students in an after-school club or area-wide organization, the chapter lists many of the resources out there, in many of our cities.

- **Chapter 8: Promoting Change in Schools.** Finally, we'll explore the strategies and challenges for teachers who want to promote more social action learning in their schools. All too often, teachers carry out projects like those in this book completely on their own. But while all of us have full plates serving our students well, sharing the effort with partners can make life far easier. Imagine what it could be like if a whole grade level, or a whole school, took on community improvement efforts. The work of initiating such collaboration is akin to community organizing. We'll outline some steps, large and small, to get started.

Educators know all too well the tremendous pressures squeezing out the time and resources and support for the kind of teaching and learning described in this book. Principals and teachers worry that their jobs can be at stake if test scores don't go up. Days and weeks of rote test prep are required in many schools. Some education journal articles even criticize extended study projects as undesirable because they (supposedly) do not include enough concentrated analysis of a few isolated skills and readings. So teachers may need to get creative about scheduling, "teach between the cracks," or substitute a project for a more traditional unit to cover the same concepts in a more active way. Or draft justification statements to explain how their projects are indeed covering Common Core standards (really—we've read some). Fact is, teaching and learning with social action can take place in just about any school.

You and your kids can do this work, too. Now, let's get started.

1
~

CHOOSING AN ISSUE

At Park Forest School in State College, Pennsylvania, three fifth graders came to be known as the "Salad Girls." They were frustrated that, due to food allergies or religious beliefs, they could not eat the cafeteria's lunch salad, which contained cheese and meat. At first they wanted to go all out and picket the lunchroom, but the principal convinced them to start by gathering information. They conducted surveys in all the classrooms about students' views on the lunches and met with the cafeteria manager, who explained that federal rules required protein in the salads—ergo meat and cheese. Undeterred, the girls gave a PowerPoint presentation for the district cafeteria manager, who agreed to pilot several salad alternatives at the school. Their effort gained the attention of the state secretary of health, officials at Pennsylvania State University, and the local news media. While this action changed only a small part of their world, and only for a brief period, the students had discovered the power of their voice. There are times when an issue for action bubbles up as naturally as it did for these fifth-grade students. However, when you want to get an entire classroom of students on board with an action project, it's not often that a single issue will spontaneously capture every student's heart. Helping students identify meaningful issues to address can provide a major learning process in itself. In this chapter, we'll take a close look at how the fifth-grade teaching team at Park Forest School helps students to collaborate, support one another, and find issues they can learn from and act on. Then, we'll consider strategies to help students of all ages to do the same.

CHOOSING AN ISSUE IN FIFTH GRADE AT PARK FOREST SCHOOL

Witnessing the Salad Girls' courage and initiative helped the fifth-grade teachers at Park Forest to go further and lead projects on responsible student activism and community involvement with all their students. These three teachers—Jennifer Cody, Elizabeth Cullin, and Lori McGarry—already shared a passion for promoting student voice, enacting democratic values in their classrooms, and developing students' sense of community. A Project Citizen workshop on learning with social action provided further inspiration and valuable structures to help them organize the work. Here, we'll see how their team collaborates in thoroughly preparing the students so they are ready to thoughtfully research, write about, and in many cases take action on social issues.

Building Community First

The three teachers begin with a series of well-planned and engaging community-building activities. Students need to take responsibility for their own supportive classroom before they try to make improvements elsewhere. One of the teachers' favorite activities is "bucket-filling," based on the popular children's book *Have You Filled a Bucket Today: A Daily Guide to Happiness for Kids* (McCloud and Messing 2006), which aims to help children appreciate the effects of their actions and words on others. Students learn about and practice filling their own and others' attitudinal "buckets." They add to their own and each other's buckets through kind and supportive acts for one another, but they can also lose from their bucket when they do or experience something hurtful. Students jot slips complimenting and encouraging one another and deposit these in decorated paper-bag buckets tacked to a classroom bulletin board (see Figure 1–1). At the end of each week kids take their collection of slips home to savor the messages they've received.

Figure 1–1 Park Forest Students' "Buckets" for Receiving Compliments

Going deeper, the teachers help students explore and compare their identities with a "stepping over the line activity." (Versions can be found on numerous websites. One especially appropriate for students is at www.freedomwritersfoundation.org/lesson-plans /lesson-1.) Students form a circle and remain silent during the activity. As the teacher calls out various characteristics or experiences, students step forward when one applies to them, and then step back. Anyone can pass if he or she doesn't wish to respond to a particular item. The statements begin very simply:

- I have blue eyes.

- I have brown eyes.

- I have black hair.

- I have blonde hair.

- I am a first-born child.

And so on. Statements then advance to aspects of students' lives—though the teachers strongly advise using good judgment about what is acceptable in any particular community.

- I come from a two-parent home.

- I come from a one-parent home.

- I have been bullied.

- I have seen someone bullied.

- At some time in my life, I have been treated unfairly or unjustly simply due to who I am or the color of my skin.

- I have been treated unfairly due to my gender.

- I have witnessed or treated others unfairly based on who their friends are, or their social clique.

These are just samples of the many questions that can be asked.

Afterward, students reflect and those who wish can share stories related to their responses. This exercise helps students appreciate the wide variety of experiences in the room, along with their own identities, even when the class appears to be a homogeneous group. As one boy explained, "You come to school thinking that everyone around you has an OK life, but then you begin to see that it's not always that way."

On a more academic level, students explore the nature and purposes of government as part of their social studies learning, and this too helps establish community. The students plan a constitution for the "island" that is their classroom, creating their own rules for how they want to relate to each other.

As a result, students become wonderfully empathic with one another. This was especially apparent one day as the students were listening to each other's presentations on a science inquiry project. On a couch to one side sat a girl next to a somewhat distracted-looking boy, holding his hand and patting it. The teacher explained later that the boy was autistic, and all the class took responsibility to calm him and take care of him.

Looking Out into the World with Critical Awareness

Once the classrooms are on a secure footing, students begin to explore the concept of stereotypes, since these will often come up in the news articles they read as they consider issues to address. Working in small groups, students look up a definition of the word, discuss it, and identify times when they think they've observed it or perhaps experienced it themselves. This serves as both an extension of the community-building effort and a preparation for critical reading of research material. Then, by comparing reports on an issue from various sources—news on Ebola as it is covered in China, West Africa, Dallas, and their own local paper, for example—the students become increasingly discerning as readers (see Figure 1–2).

Figure 1–2 Park Forest Students Reading News Articles in an "Article Pass"

The students continue to read a variety of news stories and watch short clips from CNN Student News, with the goal now of learning about issues and events that might become focuses for their investigations, writing, and action. The teachers prepare the kids carefully for this by guiding them to brainstorm about what a "current event" is, listing various news media, looking at how news articles are organized, creating a list of categories that identify various types of current events, and developing an understanding of which are more global or local.

Kids love the newspaper reading, and when a fresh stack of papers arrives, they dive at them like fish in a feeding frenzy. As one student, Ryan, commented, "There are a lot of conflicts in the world that I didn't know about. I like feeling more informed." With this kind of involvement solidly established, reading shifts to local newspapers and immediate issues closer to home. The teachers have found that projects focused on local concerns are more likely to lead to practical actions and solutions and to yield results.

Introducing the Project

Now these students are ready to start work on their projects, dubbed CHIRPs (Current Human Issues Research Projects)—individually created websites that form the repositories for their research and writing. A letter to parents, shown in Figure 1–3, provides a checklist that outlines the projects. While the project's genre requirements and assessment rubric are steeped in required standards, the letter that the team sends home to families clarifies their highest goals—to "help students . . . better understand the complexities of social issues."

Figure 1–3 Current Human Issues Project Letter to Parents

Name _____

CURRENT HUMAN ISSUE PROJECT (CHIRP) CHECKLIST

A Multi-Genre Writing Adventure
The completed project is due on FRIDAY, MAY 22, 2015.

Dear Families,

Room 210's fifth-graders are about to embark on a writing adventure, which will require months of diligent research and writing work. Each student will create a Google Site focused on a topic related to a current event or issue that is of great interest to him/her. This project will enable students to "show what they know" about narrative, informational, persuasive, and poetic writing through a high-interest topic and an authentic "publication." It will also serve as the culmination of our yearlong writers' workshop.

I would like you to help your child brainstorm a current event/ current social issue that concerns or interests him/her. Topics may range from a local issue in our school district or community to a state issue that your child has seen on the news—and anything in between. My goal is to help students delve more deeply into the "people problems" that gnaw at them and better understand the complexities of social issues as they work to develop their critical thinking and writing skills. As a class, our research lessons will focus on four key questions:

- What is the problem you wish to study, and why is it a problem (what are the competing needs/values that cause people to disagree)?

- Who is responsible for addressing the problem (government, private citizens, etc.), and what is their current policy or approach?

continues

Figure 1–3 *Continued*

- What alternative policies or approaches to the problem have been tried or suggested, and what are some of their pros and cons?
- Based on your research, understanding of the problem, and point of view, what policy or approach would you recommend and why?

On the next page of this letter, you will find a copy of the checklist that students will receive in class. This list provides students with multiple checkpoints along the way to help them manage incremental progress toward their final goal. Completed websites will be due on Friday, May 22nd so that all students may share their finished work with peers and celebrate their success.

Much of the research, planning, and writing (including student/teacher conferences and peer editing) will be completed in school. However, students may need to complete some work at home in order to meet assignment deadlines. In this case, students will be responsible for bringing handwritten or printed notes back and forth and/or working in Google Docs, if preferred.

We are all excited to begin this adventure together, and we appreciate your support. Please let me know if you have any questions or comments!

Sincerely,

As you can see, the guidelines for this project do not *require* students to take meaningful action in the world, although many of the kids do. It's clear that the teachers are aiming for the kinds of thinking that will help students to take action as they grow older: finding issues that are of real concern to them, identifying the people who can affect the most change in relation to those issues, assessing potential solutions, taking a stand, and perhaps urging others to take action. For a ten- or eleven-year-old, these are important steps, even if they are not yet accompanied by real-world action.

As they read more news articles on local events and issues, students list in their individual Google Drive folders three issues that particularly intrigue them, starring the one they care most about. While the students brainstorm topics together to generate possibilities, they choose their own individually, rather than in groups or as a whole class, since the teachers find that kids become more committed to their efforts this way (see Figure 1–4). The students do share their ideas, however, to help inspire one another.

Figure 1–4 Jen Cody's Class Brainstorm of Important Topics

CLASS BRAINSTORM TOPICS

- Breast cancer
- Christmas stockings for troops
- Drug problems in the area—especially heroin
- Recycling in the community (already lots being done in the school)
- Deforestation in the area
- Jump-Rope for Heart (fund-raising sponsored by the American Heart Association)
- Reducing the cost of college
- Homeless kids in school
- Bullying

EXAMPLES OF INDIVIDUAL TOPIC CHOICES, FOLLOWING THE BRAINSTORM

- Bullying
- Child abuse
- Cost of college (President Obama's plan)
- Providing extracurricular opportunities for children of low-income families
- Overcommercialization of land
- Struggles faced by homeless children
- SPCA
- Helping students with special needs in the classroom
- Homelessness
- White-nose bat syndrome

The teachers meet with individual students or review the choices in their Google Drive folders to ensure they are headed in productive directions. They check to see if topics are sufficiently local so that students can connect concretely with them. And sometimes the conferences reveal sensitive issues. In one case, a student explained that he wanted to work on child abuse because he himself had been abused at an earlier age. Surprised and worried about family sensitivities, the teacher asked whether this would be acceptable for his mother, and he replied that he had already obtained her approval.

You'll notice that some brainstormed topics are one-off community service efforts—like stuffing Christmas stockings or Jump-Rope for Heart (fund-raising for the American Heart Association)—rather than projects that call for actual social change. While this book generally emphasizes the importance of a more structural action step, Jen, Lori, and Liz accept service activities as legitimate for fifth graders. Many of the kids do in fact tackle structural improvements in the community, but these teachers find that service activities still provide plenty of experience in organizing an effort to make something happen in the world beyond the classroom walls.

After brainstorming possible topics, each student interviews family members to obtain their perspective on the student's topic choice or choices—thus establishing a connection of their work with the outside world from the very start (see Figure 1–5).

Then they complete a written CHIRP "defense" to be presented orally, with questions and suggestions offered by the rest of the class. The defense generally includes the following parts (though as with so much of this work, the teachers usually have the students brainstorm a list like this themselves):

1. What is your topic?

2. Why do you care about it?

3. Who will be helped because of your research?

4. Why is it important? (facts/data)

5. Can you make a change in the situation?

This year, Jen Cody's students presented their defenses to eighth-grade students at the neighboring middle school who are studying law and social justice. At this point, students' enthusiasm in their work is palpable. Gabbie's CHIRP defense (Figure 1–6, page 28) shows not only the depth of her commitment to her topic, but also her research thus far, and the connections she's uncovering between learning disabilities and bullying.

Even before the projects are under way, the influence of the effort begins to show in students' broader thinking and actions. They start approaching the teachers about organizing activities during lunch and recess, quite separate from the classroom work. Before she drafted her project defense on mentoring kids who deal with challenges, Gabbie began interviewing learning support teachers in the school to educate herself about how they work with struggling students. Another fifth-grade student organized a student group during lunch to participate in a walk for diabetes. That group also gave a presentation on diabetes awareness at the weekly all-school gathering where students are invited to share on topics and issues they care about.

C.H.I.R.P. TOPIC EXPLORATION

Dear Family,

In my class, we are about to begin a writing **ADVENTURE** that will require about two months of research and writing work. As you know, I have a topic related to a current event or issue that interests me. This project will involve research as well as informational, persuasive, and narrative writing. We are calling the project the "**C.H.I.R.P.**" or Current Human Issues Research Project!

This year, we have been learning about current events and thinking about problems in our community, region, state, and nation. The following issue is of concern to me:

Measles — and vaccinations for measles

This issue interests / concerns me because:

It could affect someone near me. It concerns me because parents aren't vaccinating their children and are putting others at risk to getting measles.

Does this issue affect our family directly or indirectly? Does it affect the way you vote or other decisions you make?

We are all vaccinated so it probably indirect affects us. The outbreaks like Disney Land makes me not want to go there. It makes me concerned about going to places with a lot of people.

Now I am interested in learning about an issues that interest **YOU** as well. Are there specific issues in our community, state, region, or nation that concern you right now? When you vote for local officials and representatives to state and national government, what issues are important to you? Please feel free to share up to two (I will take notes below).

Climate Change, ice melting, greenhouse ga

This issue interests / concerns my family because:

Climate Change issues would impact the way I voted. I would not vote for someone who does not believe in climate chan. If elected politicians do not believe in climate change they won't do thing to help improve the climate.

Figure 1–5 Jenna's Family Interview

The Later Stages

As kids move into the research stage, the teachers use the fifth-grade curriculum on research and argument from the widely used *Units of Study in Opinion, Information, and Narrative Writing* (Calkins et al. 2014) as an extended minilesson (maxi, really) to prepare them. This allows each class to engage in one brief round of research on an issue as a whole group so that, gradual-release style, students get ready to work on their own.

Figure 1–6 Gabbie's CHIRP Defense and Copy for Her Homepage

HELPING STUDENTS WHO NEED
EXTRA HELP IN SCHOOL

My CHIRP project will focus on partnering with students who need extra help in school to help them complete their work and fit in with the classroom community. Also I want to help other students have a better understanding when students need extra help. I want the students who need extra help be able to do/participate in things that they are discouraged about because other kids might not understand and might make fun of them.

I care about this topic because I have friends who are different than me, and I am very passionate about helping them be themselves but also be able to have the same rights and opportunities as me. I started to care about this topic in second grade and have cared ever since because all of those years I have had a student in my class that needed more help. I got used to helping them, and I couldn't help but notice other kids making fun of them and hurting their feelings just because the kid might not understand how rude the things getting said about them are.

The people that will benefit from my work and support are kids like my very special friend Nolan and some of his friends. They will be able to have fun and make friends just like any other person but still be able to stay themselves. They will also have extra support from their peers in the classroom for their school work and classroom jobs, and other tasks.

It is estimated that 160,000 kids everyday miss school because of the fear of getting attacked or intimidated by other kids and other students. That is sad and it shouldn't be happening and I want to change the fact that this happens.

I think that my work will definitely make a change. My goal for this project is to get some kids together and help them feel like they are still themselves but not let mean comments bring them down.

I hope that by reading this you care just as much as I do. If you know anybody who bullies people like this them I hope you will stick out your neck and help.

Figure 1–7 Researching for Social Action Involves Plenty of Reading

While some become quite independent, others—particularly those who are struggling readers—can get lost in all the detail and need individual support. Liz Cullin provides individual question lists to help those students focus, while Jen Cody varies her help based on students' particular needs.

As students begin putting it all together on their websites, the teachers provide mini-lessons on webpage design, and of course the kids dive in. Students send emails to a variety of audiences to draw people to their websites and some, like Gabbie, get started on promoting action.

Covering the Standards

The Park Forest fifth-grade teachers reviewed the Pennsylvania Core Standards to confirm that students' projects addressed nearly all the writing and informational reading standards. For example, each student's project website includes informational writing, with well-organized, relevant facts and concrete details on the student's issue, based on research they've done (Pennsylvania writing standards CC1.4.5A through F, plus standards on doing research). Students take a stand on their issue, presenting arguments and facts, and citing sources for their information (Pennsylvania writing standards CC1.4.5G through L). And they each compose a relevant story to illustrate the issue (Pennsylvania writing standards CC1.4.5M through R). They revise and edit their work with guidance from their teachers (standard CC1.4.5T), and it is all presented on websites the students create (standard CC1.4.5U). The coverage for the standards on informational reading is equally thorough.

Beyond the standards, the Park Forest fifth graders will remember their project experience long after other lessons have faded from memory. And the skills and content students learn will stick with them. Think back to Elizabeth Robbins' classroom described in the introduction: How many adults recall what they learned from a textbook about how a bill becomes a law? Compare that to Elizabeth's students' all-too-memorable learning when they tried to get a bill on reforming juvenile court procedures out of the Illinois House of Representatives Rules Committee.

PREPARING YOURSELF AND YOUR PLAN

Inquiry-based action learning may require some shifts for both you and your class. Students who have been in traditional classrooms for years may not be sure how to take the lead in planning, or may not yet believe they are capable of effecting change. Considering your role before the work begins can help you to put students in the driver's seat. Be aware, however, that preparation does not mean laying out the details for every step of the way. Following students' lead and addressing needs as they arise is a big part of what makes this work fun and invigorating for teachers as well as for the kids.

First Principles—Or Limiting the Teacher as Problem Solver

Most teachers enter the profession wanting to help children learn. Teachers are problem solvers with knowledge to share. And they want students to be successful. But it's especially important that kids come to see themselves as able and empowered, and this requires allowing them to make decisions and take initiative as much as possible. Most of the time, they have more abilities than people realize. This is not the same as letting them struggle just to develop "grit," an approach that can be problematic, with its "suffering is good for you" overtones. Teachers leading social action projects can help students with their inquiry and decision making by providing tools, strategies, and ways of thinking more deeply about an issue. And then, though the students make most of the decisions, if they are truly stuck or discouraged, the teacher can pose questions or provide suggestions to keep them going.

Heather Van Benthuysen, whose work is described in Chapters 7 and 8, thinks continuously about her role, even as she sits silent much of the time while her after-school Social Justice League conducts its business. For example, as the group reflected on a recent student opinion event it had held, the discussion was led by a student new to her leadership role. Heather wanted to give her space to lead but also support the process she was using. So she did speak up to reinforce particular steps the leader outlined—such as starting with the facts of what took place rather than judgments about it. And she voiced her own concern that she, the teacher, ended up doing most of the tasks just before the event began. "When we have a meeting, I am expected to participate just as the student members are," she explains. But as students brainstormed ways to increase audience participation at such events, Heather held back. She remarks, "If I speak up a lot during discussion, often students begin to think there is a 'right answer' or we need to move 'my way.' Often the energy that comes from students brainstorming is worth more than the ideas themselves. In my mind, every time I refrained from speaking it's because students were building off of one another."

Clearly, a wise teacher makes a myriad of thoughtful decisions as student activity is unfolding before them. At the same time, of course, it's the teacher who creates structures guiding and enabling the projects, and it's this balance that pervades the work throughout this book.

By Class or Individual

For choosing issues, one major decision a teacher will need to make at the very start is whether the class will carry out a single project together, choose issues individually, or work in small groups. Advantages and challenges present themselves either way. An all-class project can require careful work to get all the kids in the room on board. Simple voting can easily alienate the losers—"Why should I care about this? It wasn't my idea." Debates or other forms of competition present similar problems. Building consensus is better but takes time and strategic guidance, so we'll look at how to handle this challenge in more depth.

As the Park Forest teachers explained, they find that individual projects ensure students' commitment and ownership. The biggest issue for this option is that it takes more work to support students as they encounter challenges. A smooth-running classroom workshop (see Chapter 5) is essential for this approach, since it enables plenty of one-to-one conferences. And the Park Forest teachers want to encourage students to solve problems themselves as often as possible.

Listening Closely

Often when a teacher really listens to students, a core issue emerges. Las Vegas teacher Paula Laub experienced this repeatedly with her first graders as she learned to listen and then to encourage students to identify the issue that was troubling them, investigate it, decide together on an action to take, and carry it out (Laub 2006, pp. 11–18). She first embarked on this process when the students seemed upset one day and revealed that they were frustrated about the school library rule that limited them to checking out only books labeled with their first-grade reading level. This quickly led to student letters to the librarian, who obligingly changed the rules. For Laub, paying close attention to students and eliciting discussion about their concerns led to study and action on larger issues as well.

MAKING IT WORK: ACTIVITY OPTIONS

As the Park Forest fifth-grade team showed, building classroom community is an essential first step before any work on a project begins. The strategies they used—bucket filling, stepping over the line, and creating a classroom constitution—are excellent approaches you can implement as well. You'll read about more in several chapters of this book. Training for effective collaboration and strategies for helping to resolve conflict are explored in the Chapter 5 section on Organizing Discussions for Thoughtful Exchange of Ideas, and Reaching Consensus Peace circles are described in Chapter 6. Team-building exercises that high school teacher Heather Van Benthuysen uses with her after-school action civics club can be found in Chapter 7. The focus here, therefore, is on judicious use of structured activities that can help students to see a wide range of possible issues.

Simple Brainstorm

In *Spectacular Things Happen Along the Way*, we learn that Brian Schultz started his fifth graders on their investigation and action project with a visitor from the Constitutional Rights Foundation of Chicago, who helped the students explore problems they experienced in school. Following this visit, he and the gym teacher led the class to brainstorm problems that affected them, and though the list at first ranged extravagantly, one student recognized that most items focused on the miserable physical conditions in the school itself. This galvanized the kids around one conclusion: "Our school is a dump" (Schultz 2008, pp. 1–3, 26–29).

Some classes may need a bit more structure to jump-start their brainstorming. You can have students jot notes, individually or in small groups, in response to a set of questions:

- What would you change if you were in charge of your school?

- What would you change if you were in charge of your neighborhood/city?

- What is something that would make your school/neighborhood/city better?

- What is something that would make your life and the lives of your fellow students better?

- (based on Millenson et al. 2014, p. 32)

Then ask students to rank their lists in order of the importance they give them. Once the class starts sharing their responses, it will be time to narrow to a short list and then to either build consensus around one issue, or have individuals or small groups choose their preferred problem. (More to come on consensus building shortly.)

Note: The chosen issue may at first be extremely broad, or too global for students to address meaningfully—but don't worry. Once the research process begins, students will find a piece of it they can get their minds and hands around, and you can help with that, if necessary. But at this point it's important to respect and value the students' concerns, just as Elizabeth Robbins did with her class in this book's first story.

Browsing News Articles

The Park Forest teachers helped students develop a healthy list of issues by having them regularly read news articles from magazines, newspapers, and online publications that reveal resources and problems in their community. This can work even with primary classrooms, as teacher Erica Emmendorfer found. For her first-grade students, she invites parents to read articles to their children and the kids then bring them in—but this can certainly take place at any grade level. In some settings, the teacher may need to supply the reading materials and set aside reading time to ensure that plenty of browsing takes place.

Mapping a Neighborhood, Community, or School

The Mikva Challenge, the nonprofit organization in Chicago that promotes action civics (more about this group in Chapter 7), provides a curriculum focused especially on issues in students' school, immediate neighborhood, community, or town. It offers several ways to profile or map a community, covering all the public services, infrastructure, businesses, and organizations, thus gathering information on the assets as well as problems surrounding the students and affecting their lives. This avoids painting neighborhoods (or towns, or schools) only in negative terms. And the balance can help with the search for solutions later, since it identifies resources the kids might want to draw upon.

The following strategies can help fill in a community map:

- Invite students to brainstorm everything they can think of that exists or takes place in their neighborhood. They may need a few examples to get started—churches, the ice cream cart in the summer, an admired neighborhood resident—but like so much in this work, students can figure out most of it themselves. Added to the list can be services or resources lacking in the neighborhood. Rearrange the items in the brainstorm list into some categories to help the map make sense—parks and public facilities, stores and factories, holiday festivities, community leaders, and so on.

- Guide students to generate questions they might ask various neighborhood citizens to learn about the aspects of the neighborhood that people value or are concerned about. Unless they've done this before, students will need help preparing for interviews and surveys, so there's more on this just ahead.

- The Mikva Challenge curriculum suggests mapping that includes student-made photos, objects, business cards, organization brochures, and other material representing the features of the neighborhood. Attaching these to a blow-up map of the area can create a striking visual to help students consider the assets and issues in their community.

Even if students focus on their school or their own relationships rather than the wider neighborhood or community, these same activities can help them analyze the needs and resources involved. If students are to work on projects individually or in small groups, this stage can still take place as a whole-class activity, but instead of narrowing the focus, each student or group will choose an issue off the list. Obviously, as each aspect of a place is identified, students will often have plenty to say about its positive qualities and/or problems—so they will be on their way to identifying important issues to choose from.

Surveying and Interviewing Community Members

Especially if students do not know much about their locale, they can learn by interviewing community members—parents, church leaders, owners, and workers at nearby businesses and community organizations. If students wish to focus on their school, they can circulate surveys among peers and teachers throughout the building. Designing a questionnaire is an excellent activity to promote thinking about what's important for a community or school to thrive. But it takes a little work to make this go well:

- Help students get started by brainstorming with them the kinds of information that would be useful to gain from respondents. What questions will help identify issues that people are concerned about, or that are reflected in the students' own behaviors and attitudes?

- The wording of questionnaires and surveys greatly influences how people respond, so a minilesson on this topic can be especially important. For a student-centered approach, ask students to propose questions and try them out on each other to see which ones best elicit useful, in-depth information. From the questions students generate, you can point out the difference between yes-no and open-ended questions, show how "leading questions" push respondents toward one particular answer, and demonstrate that inserting particular information can affect the answers people give.

- Students can then brainstorm the questions they want to use for interview guides or paper-and-pencil surveys. Since this takes careful thought, it's a good idea for individuals or small groups to brainstorm separately, so the class can compare various versions of a question. Again, students can pilot questions with each other, with parents, or with friends from other classes to check whether they elicit the kinds of information that seem helpful. And don't forget to encourage students to organize their questions by starting with those that are easier to answer.

- If students choose to conduct live interviews, it will be important for them to rehearse with one another. Practice devising follow-up questions is especially valuable to get a fuller understanding of an interviewee's responses. This will be a new concept for many students, so use a gradual-release approach: first model the practice in a fishbowl setting with a student or another adult. Then invite the whole class to offer follow-up questions. Finally, have students practice in pairs.

- Remind students of some basic interview etiquette: be polite, be sure to listen rather than debate with the interviewee, take good notes, and thank the interviewee for taking the time to respond.

- Responses to interviews and surveys will need to be tabulated in order to determine which issues are most important to the people being surveyed. It can help to include in the survey or interview guide both multiple-choice and open-ended questions, since the former can more easily be analyzed for patterns.

- The time spent working with students on the survey and interview process will afford rich opportunities to develop writing, reading, speaking, listening, and thinking skills. Keep on hand the standards you are responsible for teaching during this process, and you'll notice that you'll have addressed many by the time students have conducted their interviews or analyzed their surveys.

- Elizabeth Robbins advises students to follow a "Just One Thing" rule—that is, to ask themselves, "If I am able to get just one thing out of this interview, one thing that I really need to find out, what would it be?" They can then construct their interview around that goal, and organize questions to build up to it.

We'll explore interviews and surveys further in Chapter 2, where we address using them to delve more deeply into a topic.

Consulting Experts

Outside experts can often reveal important issues that the rest of us are unaware even exist, or help students to better understand their underlying causes. You may need to identify and invite people into your classroom, but the students themselves may well have good ideas for this—or may be able to locate key people on the web. And one visitor can be an excellent conduit to others, as you'll see in Chapter 3, when a visit to a local alderman opened doors for seventh graders at Polaris Academy.

Writing Proposals—If Students Are Working Independently

When the Park Forest fifth-grade students choose their individual projects, each must write up a proposal explaining why the issue is important, why he or she cares about it, who will be helped, and whether a change appears possible. Proposals should also explain how the issue is open to differing points of view. Students present their defense to the class and field questions to help each writer deepen the thinking about the topic. There are a number of happy effects of this process:

- Students begin to grow excited about their projects.

- Preliminary research gets them off to a good start.

- Problems or dead ends can be uncovered early, so they don't become big obstacles later.

Identifying Topics in STEM Classes

Identifying and choosing issues in science classes will likely be somewhat different from the open-ended inquiry in social studies or English or in elementary school classrooms. Science class, by definition, has a particular content focus. Choice is still important, but is narrowed. For example, as you'll see in Chapter 4, high school biology teacher Marnie Ware's students embarked on a social action project related to the group's existing community garden. Even with that focus in mind, though, her students could brainstorm to identify a variety of social and structural needs in their school and neighborhood:

- More healthy alternatives in school cafeterias

- Curriculum and family practices that engage younger children in healthy eating so they don't reject better foods when they're served

- Courses for adults on children's healthy eating at home

- Need for quality supermarkets in Chicago neighborhood food deserts

- Availability of more foods free of pesticides and hormones in local grocery stores

- City government and park district support for more community gardens

- Use of community gardens for positive after-school activities

And for math teachers, the choices are actually much wider, since numbers, statistics, and geometry can be central to many social concerns (see "Students Can Do This in Math Classes," in Chapter 4 for an outstanding example of social action in an algebra class).

Debates

Some teachers guide their classes to decide on a project by organizing a speech competition. This can include instruction and activities to help students compose and deliver effective speeches, thus addressing speaking and listening standards. (The Mikva Challenge curriculum includes extensive support for this, complete with lessons and rubrics.) The number of "sides" will depend on the initial options students want to champion. There may be just two choices or a whole list to be represented.

An important step after the debate, however, will be to bring the opposing sides together so the whole class is behind the effort—unless, that is, you are going to have more than one project going at once. Which brings up the next concern: building consensus.

Building Consensus

So your students have created a list of issues that concern them. If they are investigating issues individually or in small groups that agree on a specific choice, you can move right ahead. But for a whole-class effort, students will need to find a way to agree so that everybody is on board. And one more "if": you may be fortunate that the whole class promptly commits to an issue that energizes everyone, in which case there's no need to worry, at least at this stage. But since that's not always the case, you'll often need strategies to help students negotiate this step considerably.

Recall how Elizabeth Robbins, in the introductory classroom story, helped the class reach agreement and yet gave much of the responsibility to them:

- She handed the task to the students, asking, "Will it be OK to just go with the majority?" When the students felt it would not, she asked how they thought they could reach a consensus. They chose "four corners," in which students moved to corners of the room based on their preferred stance, discussed their preference in their groups, and reported out their ideas. She had taught and used this activity as well as several others well before beginning this project. Another popular one was the "talking circle," in which each student gets to state his or her thoughts, consecutively.

- When the "four corners" exercise devolved into a mere back-and-forth debate, she pointed this out and, again, handed responsibility to the students, asking, "What can you do to resolve this?"

- Once students proposed listening to each other and acknowledging the value of one another's ideas, they were on a better track, but were still not clear on how to identify connections among the topics they had been considering. At this point, Elizabeth assumed more of an instructional role, so kids wouldn't continue to flounder with the challenge. She reflected back to them an underlying theme that she could see was shared by all sides. This enabled the students whose topic was not chosen to see how their values would still be included, so they were able to commit to the project.

Obviously there's no simple formula for this process. A wise teacher gives the students as much authority as possible so they can own the process, but intervenes when needed, just enough to keep it on track or to help when the students appear to be truly stuck.

Unresolvable Disagreements

If you're aiming for a whole class to collaborate on one project, you may sometimes find that there's simply no way the students can reach agreement. In that case, you may need to shift gears and proceed with two or three separate teams. This is the kind of decision that depends on good teacher judgment. Knowing the students in your classroom, can they find common ground, or are some of the personalities just too strong or single-minded to get there?

Focusing In

Be prepared: debating options probably won't be over with the initial choice of an issue. The initial topic may well be extremely broad, traditionally leading to the usual teacher guidance, "Narrow your topic!" However, rather than make this a teacher's arbitrary requirement, it usually works out just fine to let students research and explore a bit. Often, as they begin to see the many aspects of the problem they've identified, they'll quickly realize that they can't handle it all at once, and will make fresh decisions based on their own discoveries. We'll get to this more in the next chapter, on researching an issue. But the Park Forest fifth-grade teachers' strategy of requiring a defense presentation first helps ensure that students will need to make some preliminary inquiries and explain what they want to do, which in turn gives the teachers an opportunity to help students whose aim is too broad or who are otherwise heading for trouble.

A FINAL NOTE: BEING SENSITIVE TO SENSITIVITIES

While most action civics projects are ones that everyone will appreciate, students may sometimes consider issues that you might fear are too delicate to take on. Or your principal may be the kind of leader who worries about such possibilities, whether the fear is justified or not. Yes, it's important to let students make their own decisions, including making some mistakes and misjudgments, so they aren't disempowered by hovering adults. However, sometimes we may need to step in to avoid missteps that could lead to hostile situations. An after-school group at one school decided, based on a student survey, that their teachers needed to make lessons more engaging. While this was very likely a justifiable concern, the students had little sense of the resistance their criticism would likely inspire. The students eventually shifted their focus, making the issue moot, but this is the kind of topic that would merit careful input from the teacher if it moved forward, to help students both understand the issues involved and see possibilities for how to engage, rather than offend, the stakeholders. One possible strategy is to invite students to predict the pros and cons of possible responses to their actions, and then decide on their wisest course (more on this in Chapter 3).

When students at one high school campaigned to bring block scheduling to their school, some teachers were unlikely to respond well to kids telling them how to do their job. But these students—a mix of juniors and seniors—didn't leave anything to chance. Deciding on their focus was an extended process in itself. Their overall concerns were to build better relationships between students and adults in the school and to expand opportunities for nontraditional coursework. They surveyed fellow students, interviewed students at other schools, and held meetings with parents to hear the responses to a range of initiatives for increasing students' engagement with their education. Only after a year of exploration did they settle on block scheduling. Then they took to the web to research various options and found several schools in the city that were using the strategy successfully.

Next, the students met with the principal to seek her approval to present their proposal at a faculty meeting. Though noncommittal, she didn't hold the kids back. After their presentation they visited department meetings to state their case and hear teachers' ideas, questions, and the occasionally hostile objections ("Who are you to tell me how to do my job?")—which they handled with surprising calm. They conducted follow-up meetings with departments to address issues that had been raised. They visited classrooms to describe the approach and survey students more specifically. They made clear to all that they advocated this change because they wanted a more college-like experience, and more connection with their teachers. As a result of this extensive work, the majority of faculty recognized that the kids were serious and felt they should at least give the request real consideration. The result was that in the spring of the following year, the faculty adopted a block scheduling plan, and the school continues to use it five years later.

As this example shows, it's not so much choosing and studying an issue, but the actions students plan that can either stir unhelpful controversy or cope effectively with it. But if the students still don't realize the challenges, your own best judgment as the adult in the room can guide whether you need to intervene.

A final thought: While helping students choose an issue to take action on may be a longer and more complicated process than simply assigning a topic, the benefits of working through this process and empowering students will pay off exponentially in terms of engagement, stamina, and positive change—both in your students and in the world they encounter beyond the classroom. After all, that's what this work is about.

2

RESEARCHING
THE ISSUE

At Farragut Career Academy High School in Chicago, history teacher Jean Klasovsky's students began choosing their action project as many do, carrying out some initial online research, then conducting soap-box speeches and debates to argue for their preferred issues. Students in one class, after brainstorming a long list of possibilities, narrowed their choices to the impact of gangs, drugs, or violence on students—not unusual for urban teenagers. However, their very first debate on teen struggles lurched to a halt when one student interrupted with honest frustration, "This is a waste of time! There's nothing we can do about these big problems," and the rest of the class promptly, depressingly, agreed. The work came to a standstill.

Jean acknowledged their discouragement, but then asked students to think of occasions when they had observed someone helping to turn struggling young people around. This brought their attention to positive influences in some students' lives—supportive parents, activities kids cared about, sometimes a teacher. They realized that these were strategies they could learn more about and perhaps promote through some targeted action. Now students' research was focused not just on achieving the absence of a problem, but on the presence of positive solutions that already existed.

In this chapter, we'll see firsthand how Jean's careful guidance of her students' research helps them to consider new perspectives and lays the groundwork for action. Then, we'll explore strategies for encouraging this kind of meaningful and constructive research with your own students.

RESEARCHING AN ISSUE AT FARRAGUT CAREER ACADEMY HIGH SCHOOL

In the opening account, Jean Klasovsky redirects her students' frustrations masterfully—but how did she know how to do that? Jean credits design thinking—a relatively new kind of inquiry process. But what is that? Surely we're not talking about designing automobiles or couture. In this use of the term, *design* is an innovative approach to problem solving for complex human activities. As Italian design expert Ezio Manzini explains it:

> [*The key to design thinking means I change*] *from saying "What can I do to help people change behavior?" toward the discovery that a lot of people (even if they aren't yet so visible) had already changed, and in a good way, their behaviors. And that therefore, the right question is: "What can I do to trigger and support these new ways of thinking and doing? How can I use my design knowledge and tools to empower these grass-roots social innovations?" (Brooks 2011)*

Jean learned about design in a workshop provided by the Chicago-based Greater Good Studio, an organization that builds capacity for innovation across the social sector (www.greatergoodstudio.com). The approach is based on "appreciative inquiry," the process of finding possibilities in a problematic situation, rather than just dwelling on obstacles or conditions that cause it, and drawing on those possibilities to craft a solution to the problem (a strategy first described by Cooperrider and Whitney 2001). Design thinking helped Jean's students set positive goals and organize their research, as we saw above.

Naming Positive Outcomes

With the class more ready and hopeful, Jean invited her students to work in small groups to articulate some positive outcomes—that is, to state more specifically what it would look like, what would be the result, if every teenager in the school had a positive influence of some kind in his or her life. Some goals the groups envisioned:

- Children would be able to walk through their neighborhoods with their heads held high.

- Students would be healthy in mind and body.

- Every student would be involved in something he or she cared about.

- Every student would have the confidence to achieve his or her goals.

- Every student would graduate from high school.

- All would contribute to the good of the community.

After reporting their statements, the groups went back to work developing questions that could guide their research and lead them to find positive actions in their community that were taken by some adults and felt by some students. The groups drafted questions like these:

- What would allow parents to spend more time with their kids?

- What does a positive relationship between a teen and an adult look like?

- What do kids do to connect better with parents or other adults?

- How do some adults influence students to graduate from high school and go to college?

- What kinds of goals do students strive for?

- What do some teenagers do to keep themselves healthy?

The students now had a basis for planning and carrying out their research, seeking examples of success as well as challenges in their community.

Introducing and Conducting the Research

Helping students to use the next steps in a design approach, Jean asked them to plan and conduct three kinds of research: interviews (of both students and parents), surveys, and observations. Specific lessons helped the students with each method.

For **interviews**, Jean shared a short video of on-the-street interviews about whether people thought gays chose their orientation or were born with it. The interview included an unexpected and interestingly loaded question—"When did you choose to be straight?"—which made the interviewers' beliefs very clear. (View the video at www. upworthy.com/watch-these-straight-people-answer-a-question-gay-people-have-been -asked-for-years-6.) This raised for students the challenge of when and how to word questions neutrally. Students discussed characteristics of good interview questions (see Chapter 1), brainstormed their own questions, and tried them out on one another to see which ones worked best. Then they wrote each question on a single sheet and taped the sheets to the whiteboard where everyone could compare them, move them around, and decide on a logical order, with easier questions first and more challenging items later—a visual approach to analyzing information promoted by Greater Good Studio (see Figure 2–1). Finally, after Jean led a minilesson on interview etiquette, students practiced conducting the interviews with one another.

The process was repeated for designing **surveys**. Lessons on creating survey questions were similar, helping students to seek meaningful information and word their questions effectively—the main difference being that interviews can more easily accommodate in-depth answers, while surveys usually employ multiple-choice or short-answer questions that are more easily tabulated to spot patterns. In the spirit of the design process and appreciative inquiry, students included questions for parents and other adults about how they communicated with teenagers, and questions for fellow students about whether and how they felt supported by various adults in their lives. This would enable them to probe for success stories to help guide their action plans later.

Through **live observations**, students planned to see whether and how teenagers experience positive influences. They would observe and take notes on interactions between teachers and students during the school day, or observe brothers or sisters talking with their parents. A big challenge for this kind of data gathering is to focus accurately on what is being seen and avoid assumptions that go beyond the actions or conditions taking place. So Jean gave the students a chance to test their powers of objective observation by projecting a picture on the whiteboard showing a group of people sitting around a table, heads bowed, with odds and ends of food and drinks before them. She

Figure 2–1 Studying Notes and Photos to Analyze Information

asked students to describe what they saw as accurately as possible, and then helped them distinguish between interpretations and actual observations. Yes, their heads are bowed, but there's no way to know whether they are praying, mulling over their thoughts, or feeling discouraged. There are papers on the table, two of which appear to be copies of the same typed information, but we don't have enough data to know whether this is a committee meeting of some kind. Of course, in an actual observation, the purpose of the gathering might have emerged, but the kids got the point: they couldn't make assumptions to fill in uncertainties in an observation—they needed evidence.

Each student collected at least one instance of each research type, and reported out his or her data with summary statements on large notecards and sheets of butcher paper. In addition, while students worked on their research, Jean introduced a collection of crime statistic charts for their immediate neighborhood (available from a local newspaper website) and some national data, and posted them around the room for students to review in a gallery walk. The kids were of course both fascinated and disturbed by the numbers that reflected the reality of their lives. They drew a variety of inferences from the charts, such as:

- Violence increases when teens take drugs.
- Violence decreases in cold weather.
- Violence decreases when kids are in school.
- Violence decreases when students have mentors.
- Violence increases for people ages sixteen through twenty-five.
- Not feeling valued as a family member increases violence.

Jean found that the students needed considerable help interpreting the charts, so this also became a valuable math lesson on that skill.

Now, following the design process, students analyzed the research and information they'd gathered to look for patterns or trends. They found that some of their own suspicions were confirmed about the disconnect between teenagers and their parents and other family members, and they concluded that:

- The availability of advice from family members reduces negative behavior.
- Parents vary in the extent to which they teach kids to be independent of peer pressure.
- The presence of parents after school affects children's involvement in crime.

They heard from parents who said they didn't know how to connect with or talk to their children, as well as several who said they did. Students reflected about parental influences on their own behavior as well.

The Later Stages

Once the research tasks were completed, groups presented their findings. Based on the information, the class brainstormed possible actions they could take. Based on examples of positive behaviors that students uncovered, they began to pose questions about possible solutions. In Greater Good Studio's design practice these begin with the phrase *How might we* . . . . Students listed those they considered most important:

- How might we increase parents' ability to connect with and trust their kids?

- How might we help people feel safe and comfortable talking about violence in the community?

- How might we provide information to kids to enable them to be both safe and yet social on their way home from school?

- How might we let adults know what it takes to be a positive influence on students' lives?

These were goals the students would not have considered without the research they had conducted. Small groups identified the action they liked best and created a proposal for how to carry it out. This forced the kids to consider the logistics and challenges of carrying out a large-scale project. Ultimately, the class settled on creating a website that provided tips on how adults can talk effectively with teenagers and that included a calendar of family-centered community events.

PREPARING YOURSELF AND YOUR PLAN

Guiding students as they research issues without totally directing the process yourself will require you to continue to limit your role as a problem solver, just as in the issue-choosing stage of this process. Following are some suggestions for how to provide continued guidance as well as make this kind of work feasible within the constraints of your schedule and assessment requirements.

How Much Structure and Guidance to Provide

The classroom stories in this book highlight ways for students to make as many decisions as possible themselves. But they also offer structured steps and strategies for helping them with their efforts, as in the design process described in this chapter. Your best judgment about your students will guide how to balance these two aspects of the work. A minilesson on creating good research questions may be very helpful and provide skills that will be extremely useful for their future work. However, it is easy to underestimate what students can achieve on their own, so it's never a bad thing to invite students to brainstorm their own solutions to challenges along the way, to make their own plans, and to hold off assisting except to provide skills, ways of inquiring into the roots of an issue, or strategies to help when students are seriously stuck or discouraged.

When students in Alcott College Prep's Social Justice League (featured in Chapter 7) conducted visits to the school's homerooms to get input on a project, they failed to organize it thoroughly, and considerable confusion resulted about who should go to which rooms. Afterward, the teacher, Heather Van Benthuysen, invited them to reflect on how they could have handled it better, and the team was eager to do a better job. When the time came to plan steps to obtain sign-ups for the next event, one team member walked the group through a careful planning process, making sure that every aspect of the activity was addressed. Heather was not even present for this. The pride that the kids felt was palpable, and the key was thorough reflection after the activity. Heather initiated that reflection but it was the students who provided the solutions.

There is no single clear, determining factor for when to structure work for students and when to allow them to make their own decisions or even mistakes. Like each of the teachers described in this book, you must strike your own balance between teacher guidance and student initiative.

Fitting a Project into Your Schedule

Jean Klasovsky is a history and social studies teacher. She has a curriculum to cover. How does all this work on a social action project get done, along with everything else she needs to teach? Jean decided this learning activity was important enough that she had to make time for it. She wanted to make sure history lessons weren't abstract and disconnected from her students' lives. The project would enable them to find connections between their own lives and people's struggles in the past. So every Friday for much of the year—except during mandated test-prep times—was devoted to the project. The class could easily have used even more, but some time spent engaged in real-world action was better than none.

Every school and classroom is different, of course. Elementary teachers can fit various parts of a project more naturally into the periods allotted for particular subject-area study, as the Park Forest fifth-grade teachers did in Chapter 1. A school that emphasizes inquiry projects, like the Polaris Academy that you'll read about in Chapter 3, or an algebra class at the Science Leadership Academy, described in Chapter 4, readily incorporates the kind of learning explored in this book. But if your schedule is tight, project tasks can be brief—as Jean arranged by having each student collect just a few pieces of data.

And if you need to defend this use of time to administrators, remember that sometimes people need to be educated in just how much rigorous academic work is involved in action inquiry. Be shameless: pull out your copy of the standards in your state, along with your district's mandated curriculum, and create a list of the requirements covered by the various steps in your students' project.

Wondering How to Assess It All?

Actually, this needn't be a great worry. Teachers have certainly become adept at creating their own rubrics, based on the content and/or particular skills they are helping students to learn. When it comes to grading for curricular requirements or progress with standards, there is enough reading, writing, speaking, and listening embedded in this research stage to support rubric-based formative (or, if necessary, summative) assessment. However, there are some larger goals for students' learning and mindsets, and it makes sense to employ some measures to confirm that students are meeting them. These may not seem like traditional content learning goals, and you'll need to have students write in response to questions you put to them, but they're important nonetheless. Assessing growth in these areas often involves having students reflect on their own perceptions and write in response to questions you put to them. You'll find more detail in Chapter 5, but to summarize briefly, they are:

> *Agency*—acting or exerting influence and power in a given situation
>
> *Belonging*—developing meaningful relationships with other students and adults and having a role in the classroom and at the school
>
> *Competence*—developing new abilities and being appreciated for one's talents
>
> *Discourse*—exchanging diverse ideas and opinions to work toward a common goal
>
> *Efficacy*—believing that one can make a difference in the world, and that one has a responsibility to do so
>
> (Based on Mitra and Serriere 2012, 743)

Because students may uncover surprises or make new decisions along the way—outcomes that may well surprise the teacher as well as the kids—it's not a good idea to base *all* assessment on predetermined outcomes. This is one kind of learning in which it's best *not* to plan with the end in mind. Instead, identify points where you have seen growth or change, and consider how you can use assessment to help students to recognize their achievements and build on them.

MAKING IT WORK: ACTIVITY OPTIONS

The following suggestions provide options for helping students approach their research with fresh eyes, keep their work focused, and use resources effectively.

Using Appreciative Inquiry and a Design Approach

Jean Klasovsky found that the design practices promoted by Greater Good Studio in Chicago helped organize students' research on their issue in productive ways. Design thinking has proven extremely creative in enabling people to find and carry out solutions to difficult social problems. One example, shared in Greater Good Studio workshops, illustrates the power of this kind of thinking: in 1999 Jerry Sternin, Save the Children director for Vietnam, sought to attack the widespread problem of child malnutrition there, not by taking on the big underlying challenges of poverty and lack of resources, but by studying very poor village families whose children were in fact healthier. Parents in these families weren't necessarily more prosperous. Rather, the differences were that they served four meals per day instead of the usual two, hand-fed their children, and provided a more varied diet by adding baby shrimp from the rice paddies to their meals. The practices he observed became a program that spread throughout the country, improving well-being for several million children in 265 villages (Positive Deviance Initiative 2014 and Sternin 2009). As Jean's story shows, several features of the design approach in her classroom stand out:

- Defining a goal in terms of a positive condition, instead of just the absence of a problem

- Using multiple modes of research, including interviews, surveys, and observations

- Analyzing data from the research by searching for trends or patterns

- Brainstorming solutions to a problem using the positive starter phrase, *How might we . . .*

Setting Goals

The goals here are positive outcomes that students would like to attain, or at least to influence. In Jean Klasovsky's class, students identified that they wanted to increase the positive influences for teenagers in their neighborhood, leading to more constructive outcomes in their young lives. This required that students think not just about reducing violence but also about what a more encouraging set of conditions would look like, along with the positive forces that could lead to it. It's natural that in identifying an issue they wish to address, students will focus on a negative of some kind—the lack of healthy eating in the school and in families, the paltry resources for their school, the problematic justice system for minority teens, and so forth. But to identify solutions they can actually work on, students need to translate their focus on these pernicious conditions into a vision of what a better world would look like. More specific goals will come later, once research has given students a deeper understanding of the problem and the ways that people cope with it, both with and without success.

Generating Research Questions

Once students have identified an issue they want to address and have a goal in mind, they need to study the problem, people's existing solutions and the context, in order to decide in a well-informed way on a more specific goal and action to take. But what exactly should they research? As the design process suggests, they'll need some good research questions. Of course, each project will present its own set of conditions to learn more about. However, design experts propose some important characteristics of effective research questions:

- *Study the solution, not the problem.* Example: "How have high school juniors gotten back on track?" rather than "How have juniors fallen behind?"

- *Understand today; don't start with tomorrow.* Example: "How do juniors plan for college?" rather than "How can we help juniors plan for college?"

- *Start with the user, not the system.* Example: "What motivates juniors to come to school?" rather than "How does our school meet juniors' needs?"
  (Based on Greater Good Studio, "New Frontiers Innovation Lab")

As we saw with Jean Klasovsky's class, their key questions took these guidelines to heart:

- What would allow parents to spend more time with their kids?

- What does a positive relationship between a teen and an adult look like?

- How do some adults influence students to graduate from high school and go to college?

More on Interviews and Surveys

Once research questions are articulated, it's time to make plans for gathering data, and for many issues, a good source will be interviews and surveys of people who deal with the problem students are addressing. Students are likely to need plenty of help creating a good set of interview or survey questions, as well as actually conducting the processes. Some strategies for helping students gather information from live subjects were outlined in Chapter 1—research being an activity needed at almost every stage of a social action project—but it helps to go a little deeper here. Now that students are focused not only on a specific issue but also on solutions some people have devised, their questions can help them dig more deeply. This is when design thinking and appreciative inquiry become especially valuable.

Kinds of Questions

One step is to help students become aware of a variety of kinds of questions:

- Factual questions, such as a person's age or job

- Yes-no and agree-disagree questions

- Open-ended questions about opinions or experiences

- Rating questions—"On a scale of one to five, how important do you think . . . "

- Ranking questions—"Of the following five things, which affects your neighborhood most, which is second . . . "

- Multiple choice questions—"How did you hear about the sweep-and-greet program?" __Facebook __Flyer __Word of mouth . . . (mainly for written surveys)

- Check-all-that-apply questions (mainly for written surveys)

- Hypothetical questions—"If the park were cleaned up and new basketball courts put in, how often do you think . . . "

Survey Monkey and other such websites provide information and options on question types. But how might you introduce these options to students so they understand the pros and cons for each type? One good way would be to have your class look at an interesting questionnaire together and figure out the types themselves. You can find a wide variety of sample surveys on the Survey Monkey website—but be sure to use one that has a variety of question types.

Organizing the Questions

Once students have brainstormed a set of possible interview or survey questions, the next step is to put them in an order that will work well. Students may not realize at first that it's probably not a good idea to pin down an interviewee about a controversial issue in the first moments of the session. To get students thinking about this, first ask them to list some possible categories of questions based on the kinds of information they request. Then with the questions on paper strips, students can arrange them by the categories on a bulletin board (or on desks, if students are working individually). Next comes consideration of various possible orders for the groups. By this time, the students will have grasped the point and can complete the job thoughtfully.

Survey or Interview—or Both?

There are at least two big differences between interviews and surveys. One is that surveys can more easily and quickly obtain responses from a large number of people, while interviews are more time-consuming and labor-intensive. Another is that survey data can more easily be tabulated as percentages, to give a sense of general attitudes of a group, while interviews can obtain more in-depth narratives that are nevertheless harder to sum up. Again, students can be helped to make decisions about which method to use by asking them to compare results from a sample survey and an example of an actual interview. Instances of both of these can be found online. For example, student-made surveys of students and teachers about their school experience, from the organization What Kids Can Do, are available at www.whatkidscando.org/specialcollections /student_as_allies/pdfs/saa_samplesurveys_final.pdf. Also, a brief interview with Katie Couric on what makes a good interview can be downloaded from www.youtube.com /watch?v=4eOynrI2eTM.

Observations

With issues involving people readily available to students in person, visual observations can be invaluable for discovering both challenges and solutions that those individuals have already developed. In the Vietnam child malnutrition research, for example, observing in households of poor families where children were thriving revealed crucial practices the researchers had not thought to ask about, and family members themselves had not bothered to mention. So if the chosen issue relates to fellow students' behaviors—for example, after-school habits that might or might not lead to participation in school activities—observations should be relatively easy to conduct. But if students seek to influence the vote on a bill in their state legislature, observation of lobbying activity in the state capital will no doubt not be practical—though it surely would be revealing.

The following practices used by the Greater Good Studio in the design process can help students watch for specific details in their observation efforts. The vowel list AEIOU helps them remember the wide range of factors they're observing:

- **A**ctivities—the things that people do

- **E**nvironment—the space, time, and conditions in which people are situated

- **I**nteractions—how people relate to others, to objects, to the environment

- **O**bjects—the things that people are using, working with, reacting to

- **U**sers—the people themselves and those they work with or relate to, and the roles that they take on

As they observe, students can of course watch for evidence of the issue they are investigating, but they should also try to be open to surprises, contradictory evidence, or aspects of the situation that they had not anticipated, things that may offer hints about solutions. This can be quite challenging for any observer, since all of us tend to come to a situation ready to interpret what is happening based on the prior concepts—the schema, as psychologists say—that we bring to it. Ethnographers, who study the habits and beliefs of various cultures and communities, regularly struggle to find ways to see things anew rather than through the lens of their own biases. As we saw in Jean Klasovsky's class, she helped students with this by asking them to observe a projected scene and try to separate their inferences from the basic facts of the picture.

One year, Elizabeth Robbins' students decided to observe and map the racial patterns to seating in their high school cafeteria. While many students sat with others of the same background, there were some mixed tables as well. But the students pushed their observations further by rating students' social networks based on word of mouth about them, and found that those at the mixed tables tended to have less extensive networks among their own cultural group. This led the students to focus their project on teen peer pressure, rather than on race.

Greater Good Studio advises that in the design process it's good to take pictures or make sketches to record key moments in observations. This can capture information the observer can communicate vividly to others but might forget later. Then students can assemble large notecards, each with the picture at the top, a statement below it to describe what was being seen (and/or heard), and at the bottom what the students think the information means and what it reveals about the situation. This process of locating meaning in the observations is essential to making them useful.

More About Consulting Experts

Students are curious and eager to connect with someone from outside the school and it's a welcome break from the regular classroom routine. However, an outside expert may deliver information in a very direct manner, which can be quite different from a teacher's measured instruction. This is a visitor who does not give grades or control the classroom. He or she is a person assumed to have special knowledge, a qualification that kids unfortunately do not always recognize in their teachers. Of course, the kids need to be well prepared, and the process for drafting and organizing good questions is pretty much the same as for the interviews they conduct with other students or community members. They should be ready to take good notes, as well—perhaps in a two-column format with questions on one side and short summaries of the answers they receive on the other. This note-taking structure is a worthy skill to teach in a minilesson before a visit from an expert.

The Ecology Club at Prosser Career Academy High School—which you'll read about in Chapter 4—drafted a set of questions and interviewed the school's lunchroom manager to learn whether vegetables grown in their garden could be used in the school lunches, and were surprised to find that in fact she had very little control over what was served to the students. Chicago Public Schools contracts with a multinational food supplier. The local school manager is given no specific nutritional information about the food. She must serve over 1,400 students each day with a reduced staff, old equipment that breaks down, supply deliveries that are sometimes late, and corporate control conducted by the lowest bidder. What emerged was a picture of an engaging professional doing the best she could with a very limited set of resources. The information they obtained was important but not at all what they had expected.

Web Research

Consider the many kinds of information students may seek online, depending on the issue they've identified:

- Statistics describing the condition or issue

- Individuals' and organizations' attitudes and opinions about the condition or issue

- Individuals' and organizations' actions and behaviors regarding the condition or issue

- Root causes for individuals' attitudes or actions

- Laws or government regulations affecting the condition or issue

- School or government officials or structures involved in the condition or issue

- Businesses, community organizations, or school organizations involved in creating or addressing the condition or issue

- Resources for addressing the issue, and their costs

- Solutions other communities, organizations, or schools have tried

There is likely to be a wide variety of information on any one topic, some of it more relevant, some less, so you may need to help students key in on the most appropriate material. One useful tool that the Mikva Challenge *Issues to Action* curriculum offers is the "Ecological Model," which identifies the levels at which a problem presents itself, from individual attitudes to family, to neighborhood, to wider society (see Figure 2–2).

You can help students understand what each level entails. Larger societal forces, like widespread poverty or lack of good jobs, may be important, for example, but if students are addressing a problem within the school, information about those forces is less likely to yield solutions that students could usefully promote.

While there's no one formula or guideline to help students determine what information is particularly relevant to their project, a set of questions like those in Figure 2–3 can help.

As for the reliability of information found on the web—or any place else for that matter—the fifth-grade teachers at Park Forest School, described in Chapter 1, provide an excellent exercise in attuning students to the wide range of perspectives they may encounter, comparing news reports on the same event in different newspapers and other media. Young people quickly get the point.

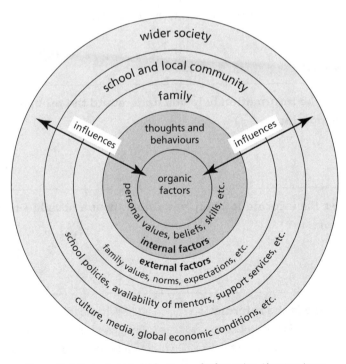

Figure 2–2 Ecological Model for Types of Information About an Issue

Figure 2–3 Guide for Students to Analyze Online Information

HOW TO ANALYZE ONLINE INFORMATION

In a sentence, summarize the information you've found. Then list important details: facts, people, organizations, concepts. Note the webpage where you found the information (so you don't lose track of the source).

How does the information relate to the situation you are investigating? (Example: If you're researching ways to improve the health of people in your community, availability of supermarkets in your neighborhood might be very important because it shows whether or not your community has healthful food options. However, data about stores in a different neighborhood might be interesting but not relevant for your project.)

How does the information help you understand the problem you are investigating?

How does the information help you think about a possible solution to the problem?

How reliable is the information? (Consider: What leads you to think you can trust it? Is the website up to date? What point of view is taken by the organization that hosts the site? Do other sources agree with this one?)

Helping Students Think About, Record, and Organize Their Information

As students interview, survey, surf, and observe, they'll be acquiring lots of new information, so it would be good to provide a few tools to help them probe it, keep track of it, and share it. As they encounter information, they can be encouraged to

- question, wonder, and dig deeper

- take notes and code information that is important, questionable, or connects to other data

- compare sources that either agree or offer conflicting information

- think about further inferences from what they are seeing, hearing, or reading

- hold discussions with partners or teammates to decide what to do or ask next, or to rethink where they are headed

A great resource to help with these many aspects of the research is Stephanie Harvey and Harvey Daniels' in-depth, strategy-filled guide to such work, *Comprehension and Collaboration: Inquiry Circles for Curiosity, Engagement, and Understanding.* One handy example is: *creating question webs* (Harvey and Daniels 2015, p. 187). This is simply a chart that enables a team to visually remind members about the various kinds of information or subquestions that each individual or group is pursuing, so everyone is clear about their task. After all, we know how easy it is for students (or anyone) to get off track or lose focus on the specific question or goal that they are pursuing. While the Harvey and Daniels book includes only a few examples of students moving into social action, its strategies will help any teacher to make the inquiry process work smoothly, guiding students to think about what they are learning, work together, and probe deeply.

How Much Research Is Enough?

School time is so very limited, and there's much to cover in these projects as well as the rest of the curriculum. Many of the topics students choose can easily balloon into a lifetime of learning and advocacy. When Jean Klasovsky saw the end of the school year looming, she asked each student to conduct just one interview, one written survey response, and one live observation. But since the class was working together, they were able to compile results in each category to form a larger total sample. The Park Forest fifth-grade teachers, whose students conduct individual projects, as described in Chapter 1, ask each student to find at least three informational sources for their research. They teach the concept of "triangulation"—checking with several sources to confirm important facts—so the kids don't depend on just one source for accuracy of information. And the teachers do quick reviews of the students' findings to help confirm the reliability of each source, since young people don't always have sufficient background knowledge to recognize faulty or biased claims. Teachers manage time the best they can.

Making Sense of It All

This is a stage in which the design process can be extremely helpful, particularly with issues that are open to immediate visual observation. A first step is to get all of the students' observations and chunks of information out where everyone can see them, and where items can be grouped and arranged to look for patterns. Have students identify the most telling observations or interview responses, write them on notecards, and post them on a wall. Invite everyone to look for visual patterns that can help the class to understand what is taking place, moving the cards around to reflect these patterns. Categories might be kinds of behaviors or attitudes that keep showing up. But then the students can begin to look for insights—tensions, surprises, or contradictions underlying these patterns, "the elephant in the room" as the design people put it. These in turn can begin to inspire creative actions the students can take. When Elizabeth Robbins' students observed seating patterns in the school cafeteria, they looked first at how these varied by race. However, they realized that in fact not all the cafeteria tables were segregated. Adding in their knowledge of fellow students' social networks led them to refocus their project on promoting student self-confidence and resistance to peer pressure.

A final thought: We've just sketched one kind of research process. But the challenge in this inquiry process—and the excitement, really—is that it can go in any number of directions. A teacher may be worried about the unpredictability, but it can always be made a deep and satisfying learning experience for students. If your students need structures to help guide their inquiry and planning, you can always adapt the strategies described in this book to provide those structures. But you may be surprised to find that your students often lead the way when you let them, by asking: What do we need to do next? How do you think we can do it? They'll provide most of the answers.

3

~

MAKING A PLAN AND PREPARING TO ACT

The seventh graders at Polaris Charter Academy on Chicago's West Side found themselves choosing an issue almost at the very start of their social action project. Of course, they did plenty of research. And their action plan changed as they grew more deeply involved in their effort. Their story began as they were studying the preamble to the U.S. Constitution with humanities teacher Francesca Peck (now the school's cultural instructional guide), generating their own guiding questions about the preamble's relevance in their lives today. They asked:

- Whose responsibility is it to "ensure domestic tranquility, provide for the common defense, promote the general Welfare, and secure the Blessings of Liberty to ourselves and our Posterity"?

- What are the gaps between American ideals and reality?

- What affects the culture of a community?

For the Polaris students, these questions were not academic. The school's neighborhood, West Humboldt Park, may be safer now than it was a few years ago, but 96 percent of the students in this seventh-grade class knew someone who had been shot or killed.

During the students' study of the Constitution, the tragic shootings at Sandy Hook intervened, riveting everyone's attention. Like so many good educators, Francesca encouraged the kids to talk about this horrific and troubling event. Until this point, the class had been exploring their questions about the constitution through responses to Hurricane Katrina, but news of the shooting galvanized them to change their focus to the gun violence in their own Chicago neighborhood.

It might be easy to write off a group of twelve- and thirteen-year-olds who want to end gun violence in their community: the issue is complicated, pervasive, and literally dangerous. However, with guidance—but not directives—from their teachers, these students were able to prepare a multipronged plan with resources and activities to promote positive changes in their neighborhood. In this chapter, we'll see how the seventh graders at Polaris gradually identified strategies and prepared materials for their effort. Then, we'll discuss ways in which you can help your students to do the same.

MAKING A PLAN AND PREPARING TO ACT AT POLARIS CHARTER ACADEMY

Polaris is not a typical school: it is organized throughout on the educational approach known as expeditionary learning. As the Polaris website explains, an "expeditionary learning" curriculum involves in-depth investigations on real-world topics through interviews, surveys, reading, and the Internet, across all grades. Students conduct fieldwork, learn from experts, and work collaboratively, leading to a final product that connects with the wider community. Polaris teachers didn't use the terms *social action* or *civic engagement*, but these concepts were clearly at the center of their work. This school, more than many, reflects the original purpose for charter schools proposed by American Federation of Teachers former president Albert Shanker—to free teachers to develop educational innovations that more traditional in-district schools could learn from.

Seeking Initial Help

Since expeditionary learning includes an action step, the seventh graders quickly decided to organize a "Day of Peace" for their neighborhood that would include a police-led gun turn-in. Math and science teacher Carrie Moy along with director of academics Roel Vivit enthusiastically joined the effort. To consult someone who could advise them, the students sent eight delegates to meet with their local Chicago alderman, Walter Burnett, Jr. As is the habit at Polaris, the class prepared by brainstorming their questions (see Figure 3–1).

Figure 3–1 The Polaris Seventh Graders' Questions to Their Alderman

1. How long have you been working with the West Humboldt Park Community [the neighborhood where the school is located]?

2. Can you tell us about some of the things you are currently working on for our community?

3. According to our research the majority of young adults [in Chicago] are either the offenders or victims of gun violence. What are ways we can get young adults off the streets or help them to make better choices?

4. What are some challenges you feel the community will encounter when trying to stop the violence?

5. What do you think community members can do to help decrease the violence?

6. What are some hopes and dreams you have for your community?

7. What impact do you think our project will have on the future?

In the meeting, Burnett gladly steered the students to the head of the Chicago community policing program, called CAPS (Chicago Alternative Policing Strategy). As can happen in such projects, though, the students quickly encountered a roadblock: this official never returned their calls. Back to Burnett for more help. This time he provided a list of community organizations and people to contact:

- The West Humboldt Park Development Council—promoting improvements in the local neighborhoods and businesses in this high-poverty area

- Neighborhood Housing Services—focused on neighborhood revitalization and home ownership

- Ceasefire—a Chicago organization focused on reducing gun violence by using former gang members as interveners

- Bryant Cross—an organizer of anti-gun-violence actions, whose Day of Peace event was featured on a TV news program that was noticed by another Polaris teacher

Revising the Plan

The students began contacting these and other community groups and decided to join with Cross' upcoming Day of Peace rather than try to start one of their own. Based on what they began learning from various activists, they decided to organize an accompanying community event, advertise it, and create a book featuring portraits of community activists as a way to celebrate their work and inform other students and the community about it. So in place of their initial plan to host a gun turn-in, the students developed a new set of interconnected steps and objectives:

- Raise funds on the crowd-sourcing website Indiegogo.com to pay for cameras, photography training, and book publishing for publishing their activist portraits

- Organize a "sweep-and-greet" activity on the peace day (i.e., inviting neighborhood residents to help with a local cleanup effort, get to know one another, and develop neighborhood unity)

- Advertise the peace day through a series of public service videos

- Visit some of the organizations recommended by Alderman Burnett to gain support and promote the event

- Write and assemble their book of portraits

As the project progressed, the teachers also invited Cross and several others to help students deal with the obstacles they would encounter and to overcome their inevitable moments of discouragement. Cross, in particular, led peace circles with the students and helped them write poetry as an outlet for their emotions. The visitors' message: even if you need to revise your plans, don't give up on your goal.

You might wonder whether these teachers were crazy to take on such an extensive effort. But as Francesca Peck put it, "We were chasing the dragon. We just continued to support the students as each step took shape." They wanted students to take the lead, but they were also ready to provide support when the kids were truly stuck. For example, when the young people set the unrealistically high goal of $10,000 for their funding campaign and obtained just $1,000, the teachers reenergized them by bringing in a community activist who helped them see that this setback wasn't a failure; it was a typical part of trying to make change in the world.

The Preparatory Work

Then came the really intensive effort. Combining student preferences with teacher wisdom, Francesca and Carrie grouped students into four teams that would take turns working on each of the planning activities to prepare for each action. Each team was led by two student project managers responsible for phoning experts, serving as representatives at community meetings, making sure the team met deadlines, and updating the teachers on their group's progress. Students within the groups worked in pairs. Thus accountability was maintained by the students themselves. The teachers and some community activists provided lessons on the following skills:

- Preparing short "elevator speeches" to introduce themselves and their project at community organization meetings,

- Designing surveys for gathering data from community residents on concerns about violence.

- Learning photography techniques from a professional photographer for the student-created book.

- Creating well-written biographical sketches for the book under the guidance of the school cofounder, writing teacher (and director of academics) Roel Vivit.

- Considering multiple audiences when drafting scripts for PSAs, or public service announcements. (The students wisely wanted to appeal not only to community members and policy makers, but also to gang members themselves.)

- Working with older students at a nearby high school to produce the public service videos.

Students met not only with community organizations but also with former gang members who worked with Ceasefire, and with a local police captain in the CAPS program. They mapped the locations of killings in their neighborhood. They met experts and activists at community organization meetings who offered help and became subjects for the students' interviews and biographical sketches. One especially valuable contact was John Groene, a director at Neighborhood Housing Services, who introduced them to the idea of the "sweep-and-greet" neighborhood cleanup activity, which they readily embraced.

Later Stages—Putting the Plan into Action

At every step students brainstormed questions and options, shared and critiqued one another's plans and writing, revised their work, and rehearsed their speeches. From January, when students returned from winter vacation, through the end of the school year, students videotaped sixteen interviews with activists and organizers; drafted, critiqued, and revised the biographies of those people; published the book honoring them; completed four public service announcements; and held their Day of Peace plus several sweep-and-greet rallies. Copies of the book were put on display in the local library; a digital version was featured in a fund-raising event by the Constitutional Rights Foundation of Chicago; and a short version can be seen on the website of the Expeditionary Learning organization at http://centerforstudentwork.elschools.org/projects/peacekeepers -chicago. The alderman ran their PSAs on his YouTube channel and included them in his regular community email blast. And the CAPS police captain informed them that on their Day of Peace, no killings occurred in their neighborhood or others nearby. (Chicago crime statistics show about ninety per year across these neighborhoods, but the students still felt good that for one day at least, no one was added to that number.)

See the Polaris Peacekeepers public service videos on YouTube:

www.youtube.com/watch?v=Y1ZObSS5UdY

www.youtube.com/watch?v=AgmBK2RGVVE

www.youtube.com/watch?v=Qtx4faNOkOs

www.youtube.com/watch?v=g3XsGps8U4A

Did the students end gun violence in Chicago? No, but their efforts may have contributed to reduced violence in their neighborhood, if only for a day. Did their sweep-and-greet activity transform the community immediately? No—their first round saw low turnout, but each following round drew more people to join them. As the students explained in a highly polished presentation on their Peacekeeper project for a national conference:

> When we started our Peacekeeper project, we thought we were going
> to change our city, but what we really did was change ourselves.
> (Boyd et al. 2013)

View the Polaris Peacekeepers talk at the 2013 National Conference of EL Education, the organization that promotes expeditionary learning: https://vimeo.com/81395520.

Students discovered that they could take action, and that adults would listen. Also invaluable was what the teachers learned: that their students could accomplish a tremendous amount, and that this could happen not through advanced planning and micromanagement but by providing structures and supports as the project grew organically.

PREPARING YOURSELF AND YOUR PLAN

This is the stage in the inquiry-to-action process when your students face the hard-nosed challenge: What can we do, realistically, to promote the changes that we want to see? The better prepared you are to encourage your students' high expectations and provide supportive guidance while letting them take the lead, the more readily will they jump into this challenging work.

Time—The Great Dilemma

While the Polaris Peacekeepers' story is a wonderful one, you may be a bit stunned by its length and breadth. Not every teacher and classroom of students may be ready for the many-pronged effort they took on. You know your kids, your time constraints, your situation. On the other hand, don't underestimate your students' capabilities or level of commitment, once they get started. Elizabeth Robbins, featured in the introduction, makes a point of not laying out all the steps at the start of a project, as she doesn't want to overwhelm young people with too much information, or indicate steps that may or may not occur as the project develops. In any case, you and they can make decisions as the effort goes forward—which is how things worked at Polaris.

Time is of course the big challenge—but don't let it deter you. Most teachers deal with this by linking project activities to required subjects, skills, or content in place of material they would have otherwise used. The Polaris seventh graders, for example:

- learned about **argument writing** and **citing evidence** through the biographical sketches

- addressed **informational text standards** through **research** for their public service announcements

- **connected informational text with other media,** including photos, videos, graphs, and other visuals

- used **statistics** through the surveys they conducted and the data they reviewed on gun violence

- learned extensively about civics and government throughout the entire project

The Polaris teachers had plenty of other subject matter to cover in the course of each day and week—history, government, reading of novels, writing (using writers' workshop), math, and science—but they linked these to the project whenever possible. Books like *The Giver* (Lois Lowry) and *Monster* (Walter Dean Myers) were chosen for their connections to the project theme. Remember, too, that the project itself evolved out of the students' study of the preamble to the Constitution. Most days students spent about an hour on the project, though a particular stage of the effort might consume more. But for much of that time students were addressing the necessary standards while taking part in an authentic learning experience.

On Making Waves

At this stage of the project, it's not unusual for teachers to worry that projects seeking change might raise opposition or get them and their students in trouble. Actually, many efforts won't be at all controversial—who could object to reducing violence and crime in a neighborhood, or to advocating for more help for the homeless? Other issues might inspire criticism, or make administrators defensive. Brian Schultz's students' letters at first drew accusatory responses from school officials, though he was ultimately rescued by the news media. No one is proposing that teachers should risk their jobs. So here are a few steps for avoiding possible difficulties.

- Keep the principal well informed. You don't want him or her to experience unwelcome surprises.

- Do more than inform the principal. Build the relationship by checking in periodically and holding brief one-on-one discussions to create a basis of trust (for more on this, see Chapter 8).

- As students weigh possible actions, help them list the pros and cons of each and foresee possible negative consequences—without discouraging them.

- Bring in experts on the issue who can share their own efforts, explain pitfalls, and describe what works and what doesn't.

- In many cases, the students will figure out a wise course of action. But if they need a dose of realism or some deeper thinking about root causes of the issue, you'll have given them the opportunity to consider the issue first, before intervening.

MAKING IT WORK: ACTIVITY OPTIONS

Some student groups, like the Polaris seventh graders, will have a goal and action in mind almost from the start. The Sandy Hook killings turned students immediately to a concern for violence in their own neighborhood, and the idea of a gun turn-in arose almost at the beginning of their discussion. However, as the project unfolded, they realized that they would likely not be able to achieve that goal. Even if students have a great idea, it's worth having them consider a range of possible options to ensure that they are putting their energy into the most promising actions, especially if an initial plan hits a roadblock, as was the case at Polaris. Here are some steps you can take to facilitate this stage of the work.

Identifying a Goal

At some point in the study of a school or community issue, students will need to decide exactly what they are aiming to achieve. Is it a change in a law? School curriculum to help prevent sexual harassment? Fresh vegetable stands in an urban "food desert"? An event or campaign to seek change in a neighborhood? A specific solution may be a natural outgrowth of the issue itself. But for some issues, there may be a number of options, with disagreement about what is needed, in which case more discussion and negotiation will be in order. (As with so many decisions, if this is a whole-class project or a collection of small-group efforts, students will need ways to develop consensus so that everyone is committed to the chosen goal. In Chapter 5, you'll find activities to help students learn to work collaboratively and to negotiate decisions when disagreements occur.)

It's helpful to invite students to consider the qualities that make for a well-chosen goal. Many organizations use the popular SMART acronym to describe these:

- **S**pecific

- **M**easurable

- **A**ttainable

- **R**ealistic

- **T**imely

These qualities help increase the likelihood of success. But most students will want additional attributes. They'll want a goal that is particularly meaningful and important in their lives and their community. And while the SMART qualities can be useful for some efforts, such as improving the social relationships in a school, they are unlikely to satisfy young people's enthusiasm to make their world a better place, especially as they are starting out on their quest. Ending gun violence was obviously neither attainable nor realistic for the Polaris seventh graders. But the teachers allowed them to discover this as they met with activists and researched their issue. It was important to support the students' passionate concern and then help them come to terms with reality, providing contacts and skills that would help them go as far as possible, rather than dictating a narrower approach.

Many possible characteristics could help define a good goal, but these might depend on the kind of problem the students have chosen. Here are a few factors to consider:

- As described in the previous chapter, design thinking and appreciative inquiry involve focusing not on the absence of something negative but on some positive action or condition that will take its place.

- Often, more immediate, local issues may be easier to tackle than larger global ones. Of course, there are exceptions to this rule, such as the project tackled by the environmental science class at Deerfield High School, which raised money to drill village wells in poor countries to eradicate disease.

- Having students think through or discover root causes for a problem can help identify a goal that is both attainable and meaningful, using a "root cause tree" graphic (see Figure 6–7 in Chapter 6). This can also help avoid goals focused only on people's surface behaviors rather than underlying conditions.

Whatever list of characteristics you and your class decide on for describing an effective goal, students can complete charts (either individually, in small groups, or as a whole class), jotting thoughts on each quality, to help define and then evaluate the options they are considering.

Planning Actions

With a goal in mind and some research under their belts, students need to plan in detail the action(s) they will take. One way to organize this is to ask some of the traditional journalist's questions: *who* will be influenced, *what* specific action will take place, *when* will it happen, *where* or in what venue or medium will the action take place, and *how* will it get carried out? Following are some of the steps students can take to get this done.

Determining Whom to Influence

In a lovely children's book titled *Billy and the Bad Teacher* (by Andrew Clements and Elivia Savadier), the child hero, Billy, lists behaviors by his teacher that he disapproves of and drafts four letters to complain about them—"one for the Principal, one for the Mayor, one for the Governor, and one for the President of the United States." This makes for entertaining reading, and the book illustrates the value of writing for thinking, since Billy comes to realize, as he lists his requirements for a *good* teacher, that the one he has actually fits all his criteria—so the letters get torn up. From our project point of view, however, only one of those letters would have had any chance of getting a result, and you know which one it is.

Naturally, students need to consider their audience carefully, which could require not only their upfront thinking but also some further research. The Polaris students learned from their alderman about a specific police department's administrator for gun turn-in projects—although they later shifted the focus of their advocacy to local community residents, even including gang members. Elizabeth Robbins' students learned in their research that the adults who could reform juvenile court procedures were the Illinois House of Representatives Rules Committee. Students in the Social Justice League at Alcott College Prep High School in Chicago (see Chapter 7) focused on increasing the social consciousness of their classmates.

The optimal way to help students figure this out—as is so often the case in these projects—is their own brainstorming. You can simply ask, "OK everyone, how can we figure out whose decisions or actions can make your goal happen? Who will be the best target of our campaign? How can we find this out?" But here's a list of questions anyway, in case students need help getting started:

- What does the goal itself call for? Some goals automatically identify their audience. A gun turn-in, for example, involves convincing gun owners to . . . do the right thing.

- What organization or governing body or leader decides on the rules or outcomes that your goal seeks to address? Your school? A local business? A national corporation? The mayor? The town aldermen?

- Who in that organization is a key decision maker? Is there a leader, CEO, principal, committee chair? Or perhaps there's an influential person who doesn't actually hold an official title (and how would you find that out)? If a governing board or legislative body is involved, there may be a whole list of people to lobby.

- Might the effort instead be directed toward a larger group—a whole school student body or, as with the Polaris students, an entire neighborhood?

- Who might be some other persons or organizations seeking the same goal? The Polaris students learned from their alderman about the community organizations that cared about their issue, enabling the students to get plenty of help.

- Who might take an opposing position on the issue? Students can think about how to communicate with those who disagree—to influence them, or at least learn the nature of their point of view. Surely no one is advocating for more gun violence—but the Polaris students realized they wanted their public service videos to speak not only to city decision makers and neighborhood residents but also gang members themselves, so they designed the videos accordingly.

Oops—More Research

While students may have already done some research on their issue, they'll probably have more to discover about their target audience. Even if they're speaking to people in their own neighborhood, they may not know about the relevant organizations and elected or appointed officials. Are the police involved? If so, who's in charge of what? Many organizations have committees or activists focused on various issues. The Polaris kids were fortunate that the alderman was so helpful. But in many cases, web searches will be essential for finding all this information. The process often continues to cycle back to more research at almost every stage. Students can be reassured that this is typical of such efforts and not a sign that their previous work was inadequate. This stage of the inquiry really amounts to a lesson—or series of lessons—in civics. But it's driven by students' desire to make something happen, rather than by a requirement to memorize governmental structures described briefly in a textbook. And their learning will include a growing understanding of the complexities, history, and particularity of their community, important kinds of civic knowledge textbooks simply aren't equipped to address.

Deciding on Actions and Strategies

Now the fun begins. Once a responsible individual (or individuals) has been chosen, how can the students influence that target audience to achieve some change or initiative? There may be many options to consider, but choosing an effective one is very much about understanding the person(s) or organization. *What* will get their attention? Letters of request or complaint? A policy study and report? A petition? If a petition, whom should the students ask to sign it? Will the responsible person or persons be open to their ideas, or resistant?

Once students identify their audience, they can become very creative with their plans. The Polaris students videotaped public service announcements, gave presentations to local community organizations, and collaborated with an activist on a wider Day of Peace event. Your students will be able to think up most of the following possibilities, and likely envision even more creative strategies:

- Letters to responsible officials

- Meetings with officials

- Reports to the public or to particular officials on solutions to a problem

- Planning sessions with responsible officials, if invited to work on solutions to a problem

- Petitions

- Presentations to interested groups

- Wider appeals through news media or social media

- Testimony at meetings of legislative committees or a school board

- Public events and gatherings

- Demonstration-style events

But how to decide among these widely varying options? Two civics education organizations, Generation Citizen and the Mikva Challenge, offer some general approaches for evaluating action. Generation Citizen's model focuses on the decision makers and other influential people, inviting students to consider how each possible strategy might impact them (Millenson et al. 2014, pp. 97–105). The Mikva Challenge model is based on the stages of a campaign for change—first raising awareness, then demonstrating support, and finally, approaching a decision maker (Mikva Challenge 2015, pp. 168–181).

Some actions are more appropriate for one stage than another, and for each there will be pros and cons. Students can organize their thinking by charting out the options and reasoning individually or in small groups, comparing their ideas, and seeking to reach consensus. As with everything else, additional research may be required, probably online, to learn more about the people being addressed and/or the history of such actions in the community.

Finally, know that every issue and every project has its own trajectory of action. Some can be contentious and drawn out; others may not involve official resistance at all, but simply a creative solution to a complex bureaucratic problem. The Polaris students' first efforts to gain the attention of a police official did not meet with opposition but simply silence. However, since their goal of eradicating neighborhood gun violence couldn't be solved through any single action, their ultimate plan was instead a collection of community awareness-raising events and communications. So the teacher's role is to provide structures to help students thoughtfully choose their actions and develop their plans.

Planning to Meet with a Responsible Leader

This is usually not a task students are accustomed to. Speeches in the classroom, sure, but meeting with an alderman? Students may have already done research on this person or group when considering whom to appeal to. But now it's time to learn in more detail what matters to this person and how he or she thinks. Students can search for news articles if this is a public official. Even if it's the school principal, it can be helpful to obtain some background information—what she taught before becoming an administrator, what initiatives she has introduced in the school, what outside interests she has. As always, asking the students to generate their own list of inquiry questions (and adding in a few items yourself if they don't think of them) is always better than presenting them with a ready-made version. A few sample questions to help get a feel for the direction to take:

- Who is this person and what are his or her specific duties and powers? What could this person do for us? What might he or she *not* be able to do?

- What are the most persuasive reasons for doing it—considering his or her position and point of view? And why is this work so important to us and to the community?

- What interests does he or she have that might support our effort or inspire resistance to it?

- What sensitivities might this person have that we should be aware of?

- What are the main things we should tell this person about who we are and why we have asked for this meeting?

- What questions do we have concerning our issue that this person might be able to answer? What can we learn from him or her?

- What questions is the person likely to ask, and how will we answer them?

- What are the next steps we can take together? What will be the follow-up to this meeting?

If this is a whole-class project, the class can discuss, research, and brainstorm answers to these questions, but a smaller delegation should be sent to the meeting. The size and makeup of the delegation is something for the class to consider carefully, since anything and everything can influence the outcome. The group should represent a variety of student points of view, and have enough members to support each other and be confident, but not be so large as to seem overwhelming. They'll need scripts or talking points. Various parts of the scripts can be drafted either by delegation members or the class and critiqued by peers (see Chapter 5 for suggestions on teaching students to provide thoughtful feedback on each other's work).

And—praise be—this is just the kind of real-world writing that students should learn to do, in place of the audience-less traditional school essays that need to be left behind.

Now it's rehearsal time. Young people often overestimate their readiness and then turn shy at the meeting itself. They may have good reason to lack confidence: many young people engaged in these projects have said they never expected adults to take them seriously. So rehearsal needs to be thorough. Parts of the presentation can be divided among the members and practiced several times with you, the teacher, posing as the official and asking pointed questions—or perhaps call in another adult in the building (the principal, maybe?) to play the role. Once again, the rest of the class can serve as thoughtful observers, both encouraging and helping speakers to reflect on their effort.

Preparing to Present to a Wider Audience

In many projects, students will discover that they need to speak to large groups—to other classes or the whole school as the Salad Girls did at Park Forest School, or to neighborhood organizations as the Polaris students did. They may decide they need to present a proposal to the board of education or their town council—let's not aim too low, here. Much of the process will be similar to that for meetings with individual officials:

- Research the audience

- Draft presentations

- Provide peer response to help strengthen the drafts

- Thoroughly rehearse

Researching the audience may be more challenging in this case, since the listeners may possess a variety of points of view and levels of knowledge. But once they are at a meeting, students can benefit from listening and discovering people and resources to help them—rather than just appearing and delivering their speeches. It was at a community organization meeting that Polaris students met the local police captain who helped throughout their project. And a director at one of the groups acquainted them with the "sweep-and-greet" activity they then used to bring local people together. So you can help students learn—and actually practice—"schmoozing" at such meetings, rather than huddling together after their presentation as students often tend to do.

Since a number of students (or perhaps everyone in the class) may be preparing presentations, students can rehearse in small groups, lowering the pressure to perform just a bit. In Chapter 5, you'll find ideas for guiding students to be supportive and helpful responders by asking questions and helping presenters to reflect on their own effort.

Creating and Distributing Multimedia Materials

Multimedia creation is a world in itself these days. While quality communication is important in getting out students' message, it's important to strike a balance between striving for a professional final product and not being bogged down by the time-consuming work. For technical expertise, the Polaris teachers called on a nearby high school, where students took courses on video creation. The teachers divided each of the four student teams they had set up into subteams—one each for concept development, script writing, and video crew. Thus the class was organized to create four separate public service videos. If these kinds of resources aren't available, consider reaching out to community members or turn to the web or books for help with scripting, storyboarding, blocking, rehearsing, filming, and editing. Here are several useful websites with school-oriented lessons on video production:

- www.freetech4teachers.com/2010/05/free-guide-making-videos-on-web.html—a site linking to free web-based video tools

- http://edutechdatabase.wikispaces.com/Cameras+%26+Video+Tools—an extensive guide to online resources for the various steps in creating student videos

- www.pbs.org/americanhigh/teachers/lesson1.html—PBS *American High* lessons on obtaining good sound and video images

Just as with meeting officials and presenting to community organizations, planning public service announcements calls for students' careful thought about their audience. The other critical piece of multimedia effort is actually reaching the intended audience. It's a great learning experience for students to create videos, but it's just as essential to get the products out to the public, so the kids' voices get heard. Most local newspapers and TV stations have a reporter assigned to education, and news people are often attracted to stories that involve kids speaking out and doing something to improve their community. Fortunately for the Polaris students, their alderman gladly uploaded the videos to his YouTube channel for communicating with constituents. This in turn caught the attention of a local TV news program that ran a feature story, helping to further publicize the students' Day of Peace.

Writing Letters

What a great writing assignment—though composing letters is likely to be one that the students assign themselves. Once again, the writers have to think carefully about their purpose, their arguments and evidence, and the audience. This is not an assignment made for exercise or a grade. It arises from students' real goals that they have come to embrace. They will readily understand that everything about their letters needs to look really good and totally competent, so revision and editing will be valued efforts, not hated chores (one of the many reasons the writing teacher/author of this book loves these projects).

While many considerations will be the same as for meeting plans and presentation scripts, one big difference is that with letters there's no dialogue, no question and answer when the message arrives. Whatever students want to say needs to be said in one go—and briefly, since a busy official is likely to have very little time to read. The writers must not only present their best arguments and evidence, but also anticipate questions or "yes-buts" the reader is likely to raise. And they need to be clear and explicit about what they are asking the official to do. If this sounds like the topic for one or several minilessons on persuasive letter writing—it is.

If students are planning to send letters to an official or business executive, a good minilesson would be to invite the class to evaluate a few sample letters by other students, to identify the elements that seem most and least persuasive and make a list of ideas and phrases that could help make the letters effective.

Working with students on this kind of writing means striking a careful balance between helping them put their best foot forward and maintaining their ownership of the work. But once letters are drafted, constructive peer response is a natural next step, leading to revisions that students will likely be happy to make. Having a collection of polished letters will be handy if they need to go out to lots of contacts—or if a single official needs to experience a minor flood of correspondence.

Dealing with Discouragement

For a teacher supporting students as they work through inquiry with social action, perhaps one of the biggest challenges is handling the obstacles and disappointment that we have seen even before actions are carried out. The fifth-grade teachers at Park Forest Elementary School (whose projects were described in Chapter 1) have found that commitment can flag when kids encounter difficulty finding good sources of information, at which point the teachers don't hesitate to help. Some students get discouraged quickly if there's not enough good information on their issue, or they realize they aren't as interested in it as they thought. The solution in that case is to choose a new topic as early in the process as possible.

Helping students to deal with challenges at whatever stage they emerge is an essential part of this work. Some steps to help:

- Invite activists to talk with the students about how they themselves persevere in the face of difficulties and reset goals when necessary, as the Polaris teachers did.

- Connect students with organizations that work on their issue, as the Polaris teachers and their helpful alderman did. Use talking circles to allow students to voice feelings about their frustrations. Students sit in a circle and take turns speaking by passing a "talking piece" consecutively around the circle, to enable deeper reflection and respectful listening (see Chapter 6). There will usually be both doubters and hopeful students whose remarks help them feel more positive about the effort. Polaris teachers found that this particularly helped students cope with conflicted feelings if they had relatives who were gang members.

- Help the students to value all that they have achieved by reminding them of the meaningful work they've done at each stage—the letters written, the meetings with public officials courageously held, and the ways they've worked together.

- And always remember that young people are usually more resilient and optimistic than adults.

A final thought: It's true that our students can't fix all the world's problems—at least not during the one semester or school year we're given with them. However, with some guidance, well-placed instruction on skills they find they need, and help discovering their own abilities and initiative, not only can they develop constructive action to make a difference in their community, but they'll be inclined to continue such efforts in the future. And you'll be amazed at how hard the kids work at it.

4

~

TAKING ACTION

By this point in the process, if you're facilitating a social action project, you've guided your students as they've chosen issues, researched, planned, and rehearsed. You've encouraged them, held minilessons, and provided structures to enable their own problem solving. Now it's their show. Like the coach at a basketball game or the director of a student play, you're now on the sidelines. You may accompany them when they meet with an official or speak at a gathering, or serve as a traffic cop as they go about their action steps, but it's their voices that must be heard. In this chapter, we'll see how the students at Prosser Career Academy High School in Chicago took action with their work, even when that action took unexpected turns. Then, we'll look at the teacher's role in this, the most student-centered stage of the process.

TAKING ACTION AT PROSSER CAREER ACADEMY HIGH SCHOOL

Just north of Prosser Career Academy High School lies a large, overgrown, and long-unused soccer field. It's now being transformed, plot by plot, into a school and community garden, mainly by the Prosser Ecology Club led by biology teacher Marnie Ware. A dozen raised plots are being cultivated by various groups—the Ecology Club, biology classes, a nearby elementary school, a neighborhood church group—and French classes under teacher Marci Dorfman are creating a French garden. Like a great many Chicago teachers, Marnie was angry as she watched Chicago Public Schools cut budgets, close schools, and reduce opportunities, especially for students in poorer neighborhoods, and the garden was one way to counter these developments. The Ecology Club garden already reflected an accomplished action for the school and the neighborhood. But as Marnie, Marci, and the students investigated whether and how vegetables from the garden could be included in the school lunches, several issues and actions began to unfold that they could not have predicted at the start.

More than fifty students belong to the Ecology Club, though a core of five or six actively guide the planning and the work (see the garden plan in Figure 4–1). They've been working for over a year to create their garden—not just for the school, but for the benefit and participation of the whole neighborhood. They hold work days on Saturdays

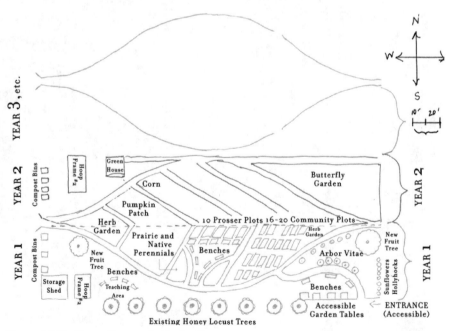

Figure 4–1 The Prosser Community Garden Plan

to tend the garden and gradually build various structures needed to care for it. Periodic open house events bring neighborhood residents in to learn what the students are doing, help with the garden, and learn about gardening itself. The first "build day" in May 2014 brought out two hundred students and three hundred community members (see the invitation in Figure 4–2). Since the school has little funding for all this, Marnie applies for grants from every possible agency and foundation that could take an interest in the club's work.

Identifying a Significant Issue

Now the club is working to use the garden to promote change in the wider school community. Students first brainstormed possible projects to do this:

- Gaining healthier school lunches, using organic vegetables from the club's garden

- Increased recycling and composting in the school

- Promoting gardens in the neighborhood

- Developing garden art to beautify the area and model such projects for the neighborhood

Figure 4–2 Invitation to the Garden's First Build Day

- Increasing student awareness/involvement in the garden and the Ecology Club
- Obtaining physical facilities (mobile classrooms, actually) to hold classes in the garden

They analyzed these, using the rubric shown in Figure 4–3 to help them decide on their focus.

Once votes were tabulated, the two favored projects were the lunches—a widespread concern of students everywhere, of course—and garden art. With vote tallies for the two about equal, the students hesitated to come to consensus. But since this was happening in November, everyone decided they would first start learning about the lunch procedures, with time to learn more about garden art later, before spring arrived. This account focuses on the lunch issue, then, with particular attention to the actions the students took. In fact, the school lunch question proved to be much larger and more political than either the students or the teachers imagined.

Doing the Research

The first step in the research, then, was to interview the school lunchroom manager, Yolanda Ortiz. The kids brainstormed a list of questions for her, then decided on the order they wished to ask them. Club member Emmanuel B. posted these on the club's Edmodo blog (see Figure 4–4).

Figure 4–3 Rubric for Analyzing Possible Garden Projects

Project	How strongly students feel	How difficult to achieve	Degree of effect on school or neighborhood	How much fun to do
Club's garden vegetables in student lunches				
Recycling and composting				
Gardens in neighborhood				
Garden art				
Student awareness				
Classrooms in the garden				

Figure 4–4 Emmanuel B. Blog Post

EMMANUEL B. TO ECOLOGY CLUB

Hello Ecology Club. Today we discussed various things we can do to bring change to the school. The main focus of the meeting was school lunches. We had decided that I will contact Mrs. Ortiz so that she may be able to attend one of our meetings. Below are some questions we collectively came up with to ask her:

1. Tell us about yourself.

2. What are the legal considerations (requirements) needed to be in a school lunch?

3. What does the budget look like for school lunches?

4. What do you know about the supplier?

4.5. Do you know where the food comes from?

5. What are the pros and cons of working with our current supplier?

6. Statistics on what is chosen.

7. How much food is ordered out and how long does it last?

8. What is the healthiest lunch option? What is healthy by nutritionist standards?

9. Levels of sodium?

10. If lunches change will the students eat them?

11. Why is special food served only once in a while?

12. What veggies from the garden will be used and how much will be needed to support the whole school?

When the kids sat down with Mrs. Ortiz (see Figure 4–5), they quickly discovered that while she was very open and forthcoming, she herself had surprisingly little information on the nutrition of the food, and even less control over what would be served. Much of the food was prepared in advance by Aramark, the large service corporation contracted by Chicago Public Schools. The baking she used to enjoy was no longer done on site. Even when cooking was required, say in making pizzas, she had to follow recipes sent by the company. And her work was constantly challenged by staff reductions, old equipment that frequently broke down, scant janitorial service, and the reality that the food was being provided by the lowest bidder. The quality of their meals, the students learned, was affected by the shrinking funds for public schools.

Figure 4–5 Interviewing the Prosser Cafeteria Manager

As for vegetables from the Ecology Club's garden, Mrs. Ortiz could only refer the students to her supervisor, an Aramark manager. Of course, the students wanted to interview this person. But first they needed to research issues surrounding school lunches so they'd be prepared. Marnie started them by sharing a documentary on nutrition in America, *Fed Up*, narrated by Katie Couric (see http://fedupmovie.com/#/page/home). It focuses on childhood obesity, dietary habits, and the marketing, political lobbying, and profit making that promotes this health problem. The cuts in funding for school lunches and the lobbying that promotes schools' dependence on fast-food providers come in for special excoriation. As the students watched sections of the film, they paused to pose a number of questions that were beginning to concern them:

- Why isn't there at least one healthy choice in our school lunch?
- Why can't we have vegetarian or vegan lunch options?
- What substitutions could make popular foods like pizza healthier?
- How much does the government invest in school lunches, and does this vary by state or community?
- What laws or regulations affect school lunches?
- What would it take to get more students to eat healthy if choices were offered?

The film helped answer several of these questions, as it explained how lobbying affected the U.S. Department of Agriculture guidelines on school lunches, and how budget cuts had led to the use of pre-prepared foods from a few large corporations in place of dishes cooked in school kitchens. And it led as well to the students' first idea for an action in the school: a screening and discussion of the film for a large number of the school's students.

Meanwhile, the political side of school lunches suddenly heated up. The students learned that Chicago's Better Government Association had just reported on the city's school lunch nutritional quality (Chase 2014). Officials resisted revealing the data until a Freedom of Information Act request forced the issue, saving the kids the considerable frustration that they would have faced in their own inquiry. One surprising piece of information was that fewer than half of all Chicago students even eat the school meals. Another revealing factoid was that in answer to a previous request, the administration had described the ingredients in their chicken nuggets as, to be very specific, "chicken nuggets." Further, the head of the Chicago school lunch program had been accused of favoritism in awarding the food contract to Aramark, since she was a former executive there.

The Chicago administration suddenly launched an online survey of students to gauge their preferences on school meals—seemingly to show their responsiveness in the face of public criticism. The Ecology Club members decided, in turn, to create their own survey, realizing that they didn't have accurate information on what their fellow students were actually eating every day (or not eating—in fact, several club members simply skipped lunch and suspected that many other students did as well). The students had moved from simply complaining about unappetizing pizza and chicken nuggets to active investigation of larger issues of health, government, and money.

A First Action Step

Watching the *Fed Up* documentary inspired the group to organize a showing for freshmen in the school, with a pre- and post-viewing survey to see whether and how the information changed students' attitudes toward healthy eating. This was, then, both an action to create awareness and a further research step to gather more data. The students brainstormed survey questions and prioritized them, working in small groups. Marnie and French teacher Marcia Dorfman provided a short lesson on types of survey questions, and students each took one question to refine so it would obtain the information they sought.

On a Wednesday afternoon in April two hundred freshmen filed noisily into the Prosser auditorium. After a few introductions and formalities, they grew silent as the film recounted the ways that the federal government cut support for school lunch programs and showed kids gladly digging into their fast-food meals. A sample of a hundred surveys tallied after the event yielded a number of revealing patterns:

- About 80 percent rated the taste of the food as fair to lacking (i.e., a 3 or a 2 on a five-point scale).

- Similarly, about 75 percent thought the nutrition was fair to lacking.

- About half throw away some of their lunch.

- Two-thirds, however, say they often eat the fruit that comes with the lunch.

- A large majority—85 percent—said they would sometimes or often take advantage of a salad bar if it were offered.

- Two-thirds would eat vegetables from the Prosser garden, if these were included in the lunch—though the other third rejected the idea.

- Students were split rather closely on whether healthier lunches would actually lead to improved eating habits—55 percent saying yes, 45 percent no.

- The postfilm survey showed little change in students' responses. About 15 percent shifted to positive attitudes toward veggies from the garden, but almost none thought eating habits would change. In fact, a few actually grew more pessimistic after viewing the film—influenced, perhaps, by the discouraging portrayal of the situation.

With this information in their heads, the Ecology Club students felt ready to set a meeting with Aramark's representative to the school—though they had learned from the survey that it would probably take more than a change in the lunch menu itself to get fellow students following a more healthy diet.

The Crucial Meeting and Next Chapters

The meeting with the Aramark representative turned out to be almost an anticlimax. It seems that Chicago Public Schools had recently ended its long-standing and frustrating policy of forbidding the use of school garden vegetables in the cafeterias. "Eat What You Grow," a new program for safe growing and handling of vegetables, had been established, along with an endorsement by Mayor Rahm Emanuel—and the Prosser Club was able to get certified for it (see Figure 4–6). Aramark would support the effort if the Ecology Club students were willing to tackle the detailed work of maintaining the rigorous sanitary process for growing and providing vegetables. The students were now faced with two big decisions: (1) whether to take on the supply

Figure 4–6 Working in the Garden

work and (2) whether and how to launch an education campaign for a healthier diet among Prosser students, in light of the survey results. But these would be issues for another school year. As the students were learning, the process of change is gradual, and the work involves many steps and stages.

PREPARING YOURSELF AND YOUR PLAN

Chapter 3 outlined many possible actions students may plan for a project—writing letters, making presentations to responsible officials, organizing public demonstrations, submitting proposals for improved school or public policies, educating other students or community members, and publicizing the need for action. A few real-world examples: an industrial technology class in a Decorah, Iowa, high school discovered that wild eagles in their area were being electrocuted by the high-voltage wires they perched on, and convinced the local electric power company to install student-built protective perches on their transmission towers. Students in a run-down Chicago school building (not the same one as Brian Schultz's, described in previous chapters) campaigned successfully to get their school renovated. Others have advocated for homeless youth, planted community gardens, or worked to improve the social culture and student leadership in their own school. Each of these calls for its own kind of student initiative, so there's no one formula for the teacher to follow, except to serve as a witness, cheerleader, and occasional support. Nevertheless, here are a few guiding principles.

Your Role

For the most part, whatever control of the work that you may have retained is mostly over now. And as is so often the case, students will step up in ways that completely surprise you. Kids who may have seemed to be barely listening in class transform into mature and competent advocates. Even if some actions don't work out, young people are more resilient than we might imagine, and they recognize that the actions themselves are worthy accomplishments. Time to reflect will come later. Enjoy this moment.

Keep the Principal in the Loop

You've already briefed the principal on your students' project, but as actions are about to take place, make sure he or she is aware and prepared for inquiries from parents, community members, or the media. Even if the effort is viewed in a positive light by everyone, you'll want the principal's responses to be articulate and well informed. If there is controversy of any kind, the principal must be able to explain the educational value of the project and assure people that the students and not the teacher chose the issue and the stance they are taking.

MAKING IT WORK: TAKING ACTION

While the students are most assuredly in the driver's seat at this stage in the process, you can support them by helping them to stay on track as the need for further actions may emerge, to value their work if they face setbacks or disappointments, and to reflect on and learn from their accomplishments.

Remember That It's Often an Extended Process

Be prepared for a project to mushroom into a longer campaign than you or the kids may have first imagined. While the Polaris Academy students' action, described in Chapter 3, was a specific neighborhood Day of Peace against gun violence, it also grew into a larger sequence of efforts. Letters to, or a meeting with, an official may lead to another step, either because the students didn't get the outcome they sought or they learned that another person or governing body was responsible. When one of Elizabeth Robbins' classes created a curriculum unit on date violence and presented it to the Chicago School Board, they learned that it would also take a separate meeting with the school's CEO to get it accepted as an official piece of high school curriculum. (The story of the students' success is recounted in Robbins' TEDx talk, www.youtube.com/watch?v=7-lUrM-rmIE.)

If this is a class project, it may stretch across the year and will be limited by the calendar. Even then, though, some enterprising students may decide to continue the work on their own. Among the fifth graders who carried out individual projects at Park Forest

School (see Chapter 1), one student who planned to keep going sent the letter shown in Figure 4–7 to the local food bank.

Another possibility–the class effort may itself morph into an after-school club. One advantage of such a club is that the work can continue from one school year to the next, as we shall see for the Alcott College Prep Social Justice League, in Chapter 7. At the end of one year, league members had bemoaned their fellow students' lack of social consciousness. But the league's continued actions the next year—promoting a "Soap Box" speech competition across the school, speaking about their activities at open house occasions, holding "Open Minds Open Mic" events for students to voice their concerns—began to visibly change the climate at the school.

Figure 4–7 Jordan's Letter

Hi Ms. Pioli! My name is Jordan Reed. I'm going to be a 6th grader who attended Park Forest Elementary School last year. This past year, I got to write a magazine about hunger in America (see attached). I really enjoyed learning more about this topic and it got me thinking about some needs in the community. Specifically, I would like to help kids in my elementary school have food on the weekend when there is no school lunch or breakfast. The idea is to put together a sack of kid-friendly food for these students to take home on Friday so that they are ready to learn on Monday. A program like this has also been successful in Gaithersburg MD (http://mannafood.org /index.cfm?page=smart-sacks) and Altoona (https://www.facebook .com/pages/Mountain-Lion-Backpack-Program/532624170105702).

Last week, I got to meet with my principal Donnan Stoicovy and the SCASD Food Service Director Megan Schaper, about the possibility of starting a program at Park Forest Elementary to provide weekend food for students in need. Right now there are over 100 students at PFE (22% of the school population) that are eligible for free and reduced lunch and could benefit from the program.

Ms. Stoicovy and Mrs. Schaper are supportive of the idea and suggested I talk to you about how the Food Bank might be able to help with this type of program. Do you have any time this summer that you could meet with us? Thanks for your time!

Jordan Reed

Students *Can* Do This in Math Classes

For math teachers Brad Latimer and Sunil Reddy at the inquiry-based Science Leadership Academy in Philadelphia (along with Erin Giorgio, who participated in the first year of the project), students' inquiry and action projects on social justice issues are key features of their Algebra II classes. The students were especially enthusiastic about the actions that put their math investigation to work in the real world. Here was their assignment:

Overview of Project
For your fourth-quarter benchmark, you will use several key concepts from our explorations of probability, statistics, and data analysis. In a group, you will focus on one major social justice–themed issue in the U.S. You may choose one of the suggested focal topics, or you may create a proposal for your own social justice issue.

Once you have decided on your topic, you will engage in research focused on statistical analysis of your topic. *All sources must be cited for this project.* Once you have conducted extensive data-based research, you will collaborate as a group to create each of the following:

1. A two- to five-minute video public service announcement aimed at educating people about your specific topic. Your video must include an overview of your data, key statistical calculations (including measures of central tendency, probability, and odds), and at least two different visualizations of your data. Your video should be both informative and engaging; you should be as creative as possible here.

2. A detailed written report, which goes more in depth into your mathematical analysis. You must clearly outline all of your relevant data in the report. *Additionally, there is an individual component for the report. Each individual member of your group is responsible for doing the following (and identifying which sections are their own):*

   a. Analyzing at least one aspect of data in terms of central tendency. This should include a focus on mean, median, mode, range, quartiles, and IQR, and should also include at least two original percentage-based statements about your data.

   b. Analyzing at least one aspect of the data in terms of both probability and odds. For this component, you should include both independent and dependent probability if possible.

c. Creating at least two visual representations of key components of your data.

d. **Bonus:** If possible, include permutations and combinations in your written report.

e. **As a group (4 or 5):** Your report must explain why your topic could be considered a social injustice and conclude with a "Future Action Plan" section. In this section, you should collaborate with your group members to create specific recommendations for how we, as a society, can work to eliminate social injustices that exist. Discuss how the graphs/visual representations might change if these interventions were implemented on a large scale. In this section, you should include as many specific mathematics-based recommendations as possible.

f. **Execution of Action Plan:** Due Friday, 5/22. Your group will work within the Philadelphia or national community to execute at least one of the recommendations from the Future Action Plan section of your report. This must be completed by 5/22, and you must have some sort of evidence of what you did for this component of the project (pictures, videos, posters, etc.). Your group will be giving a brief presentation of the execution of your action plan to the class.

Examples of projects and the actions that student teams carried out:

- On standardized tests and race—students created a website providing links to free test-prep material and circulated flyers at neighborhood schools and churches alerting people to resources their schools could not provide.
- On standardized tests and college admissions—students sent letters to college admissions officers urging them to broaden their admission requirements.
- On the death penalty—while this is a standard topic for students, this group went further, designing and presenting minilessons on the issue to freshmen and sophomores.
- A Google Drive folder with materials from this project can be viewed at https://drive.google.com/drive/folders/0B2piNgDVXKQNeDJpdm 5saGVyd2c.

Perhaps the largest, longest-running student community action project in the country, "Youth Dreamers," began in 2001 with a class of nine students at the Stadium School in Baltimore, Maryland, led by middle-school teacher Kristina Berdan. The kids resolved to create a youth center to keep fellow students off the street and out of trouble. Over an amazing nine years they persevered, raising $900,000 to rehab an abandoned house for the center, and creating a series of programs for teens. Additional students took the course in successive years and contributed to the effort, with many of the lessons in later years taught by the more experienced Youth Dreamers. Though funds have since become scarce, the project has morphed into a separate non-profit with former students on its board, guiding efforts to promote progressive education and community activism. The project has served hundreds of neighborhood youth, and changed the lives of many of the Youth Dreamers, who are now active, successful adults in their community.

Of course, not all projects will reach this level of success, but one never knows what potential lies waiting to be unlocked. Kristina Berdan testifies that a number of the original students were failing most of their regular courses even as they were growing into skilled leaders in the project (see Berdan et al. 2014; Harris et al. 2006; Berdan et al. 2006; and www.youthdreamers.org).

In Case It Doesn't Pan Out

Students are often more resilient than we expect in the face of frustration. As the Polaris students explained in their keynote presentation at the 2013 National Expeditionary Learning Conference:

> When we started our Peacekeeper project, we thought we were going to change our city, but what we really did was change ourselves. What we learned last year was this: whether you are a city who has to pull yourselves up by your bootstraps to rebuild after a catastrophe, or a school that has to figure out how to put all the pieces back together after a tragedy, or seventh graders in a community on the West Side of Chicago trying to make the neighborhood safe, what we learned was that this kind of work takes . . . perseverance and persistence . . . We could have quit when policy makers wouldn't return our phone calls about a gun turn-in; we could have quit when our Indie-Gogo campaign for our book fell short; we could have quit when not many people showed up for our first sweep-and-greet; but the fact is, we didn't. Sometimes we fall short, but we don't strive for perfection. We strive for progression. And never again will we be the

> kind of people who accept the unacceptable because [we might think]
> that's the way things are. (Boyd et al. 2013)

Brian Schultz had to deal with the outcome that his students' relentless campaign for a new school didn't get them what they so passionately fought for. When he fearfully relayed the bad news, the kids at first reacted angrily. But as a wise teacher should, he asked them to write in their journals, and there they reminded themselves of all that they had accomplished:

> "We have got heard by a lot of people like being on the newspaper and the television . . . we were a good group of kids fighting for what is right. Carr [the school] has Carr pride, and I will keep it when I go to a different school."

> "We did not do this work for nothing—we did it because we wanted to."

> "That must mean that it is time for us to go to more big and better things."

Reflecting

Whether an action is successful or not, helping students understand and value their effort is essential so that they carry the lessons and the skills they have acquired into their future. Students can be hard on themselves, too, so it's good to help them realize all that they've done. It's good to have students keep a log of the various steps and tasks that they've carried out as individuals and as a class together. Students tend to live in the present and not keep close track of what they've accomplished over a long period. The log can be useful, too, for both you and the students to evaluate their work, when the time comes for that.

Heather Van Benthuysen, English teacher and sponsor of an after-school social action group at Alcott College Prep High School (which you'll read about in Chapter 7), views reflection as one of the most important steps in the whole process. One example of its value: after the group held an "Open Minds Open Mic" event, they gathered to reflect a few days later and observed that it didn't really inspire the "civic discourse" they'd sought, but was just a series of short speeches and performances. They'd hoped for audience responses at the end, but at that point people were ready to bundle up and head home. This recognition led to a very different approach for their next effort. Using an "On the Table" format they'd learned about, they invited teachers and students to hold round-table conversations on the question, "What is the best way to achieve justice: violent actions or nonviolent actions?" Since they wanted more than random opinions, they invited teachers to lead lessons related to their question in advance, and even provided sample lesson plans—thus raising awareness and helping students become better informed beforehand. The occasion itself was of course fueled by pizza and pop, and was highly successful (see Figure 4–8).

Figure 4–8 One Group at the Alcott Discussion Event Using the "On the Table" Format

An email exchange between two student leaders and their teacher/advisor, Heather (Figure 4–9), shows just how seriously young people can take the reflection process.

Figure 4–9 Email Exchange Between Students and Teacher

Mon, Feb 9, 2015 7:33 PM:

Ms Van and Bea,

I am writing this email as an apology. I have not been very active with the OMOM [Open Minds Open Mic student voice events] project and I know I'm supposed to be a big leader in this project. I am still learning how to be a leader and I know that is evident. I have been slacking lately due to a lot of stress. I apologize. Lately, I have felt extremely guilty for the slack and practically dumping my responsibilities as the project leader on both you two. However, I want to be as involved as I possibly can because you know how excited I am about OMOM. If I have to stay extra days to plan this out, I will. I know this is only our first but I want this project to be huge! I want to see other schools getting involved with us (which they already are). Although I have these huge ideas, I just ask that you both guide me in being a better leader. I know that next year I will be taking on Bea's role and it seems like every year the shoes get bigger to fill.

Again, I apologize and I thank you guys for always being there as people I could talk to.

Kristine Hernandez

Feb 9, 2015, 7:37 PM:
Today is the tomorrow you were promised yesterday!

Life moves in peaks and valleys . . . you may have been struggling the last few weeks, but that's what good teams do—we have each other's back and help out when someone needs it. We have your back—you don't need to worry. I'm sure if the tables were turned you would do the same thing.

Thank you for your apology—you don't need to feel bad! Get motivated! We need to get some acts!!! :)

Moving forward I would say the most important thing is to be positive and excited so your energy becomes contagious to the rest of our team, and the students and teachers!

Heather Cerny Van Benthuysen, NBCT
Cc: Bea Eusebio

Feb 9, 2015, 10:36 PM:
Kristine,

No need to feel bad about anything. :) I'm glad to help out with this great idea of yours. I'll always have your back in whatever project you're gonna have in the future even when I graduate. Remember that! Don't be so hard on yourself. You've done a lot for the team. You're one of the greatest leaders at Alcott. Even though you're a sophomore, I admire your leadership and want to be as innovative as you one day.

Bea Eusebio

Feb 10, 2015, 7:17 AM:
Thank you so much Bea! I truly appreciate it (: I always look up to you in all you do. That is why I am looking to you and Ms Van for guidance.

Kristine Hernandez

As Heather explained about this exchange, "[I]t not only shows how students grow doing this work—but how powerful and important reflection is in making it work . . . and that teachers need to do it. For me this is what it's all about—truly—not the outcomes . . . the process."

A final thought: Achieving—or even just attempting—meaningful improvement in the community is something to value, especially at a time when individual success and corporate profit seem to be the prime goals for so many in this country. Just as important, seeing themselves as agents of change has a tremendous impact on students' sense of efficacy as growing young people. The community begins to perceive young people and their school in a fresh and positive light. Teachers who guide social action projects hear these responses again and again. Oh, and let's not forget that the kids are learning in a highly memorable way the academic skills called for by standards.

No matter whether students reach all of the high goals they set for themselves at the start of the project, you can honestly celebrate their achievements with them and help them realize all they have accomplished.

5

~

EMPOWERING STUDENTS IN THE CLASSROOM

Many sides of teachers' work mirror one another. If students are to become empowered, responsible citizens, their classroom needs to reflect that empowerment as well. Otherwise kids will know we don't really mean what we say when we claim they *can* make real change in the world. Why would they feel their voice will be heard in the community if it's not important in their classroom? Of course, this does not mean teachers abdicate their roles: giving students initiative and helping them succeed at work that is new to them requires the teacher to provide structures that balance guidance with independence. In this chapter, we'll look at how to lay the foundations of this work: building a strong classroom community and establishing a workshop structure in the classroom.

BUILDING CLASSROOM COMMUNITY
AND GUIDING THOUGHTFUL CONVERSATIONS

If we want students to work together for social action, their classroom must be a place where they support and encourage each other, have challenging conversations, can reach consensus when necessary, and air differences respectfully, and where harmful judgments of others—if they come up—can be sensitively addressed. Usually, this environment does not spring up on its own. Students come to school with many preconceived ideas and beliefs, so it's essential to help them be both honest and respectful. That can sometimes be a challenge, and kids need to learn how to work together and listen to one another. Meira Levinson, in her penetrating book on student civic empowerment, *No Citizen Left Behind*, describes a moment when one of her students lumps together neighborhood families who are "Vietnamese, Chinese, Japanese, whatever." When several Asian students object, he responds, "Hey, you're all Asian! Why does it matter if I call you Vietnamese or Chinese? You all ain't that different" (Levinson 2012, p. 62). When students get into real conversations about real issues, some pretty messy assertions can be heard. Even when they agree on a social issue to explore, a class or group can experience plenty of misunderstandings. What's a teacher to do?

Community Building

As shown in Chapter 1, building supportive relationships and respect among students lays the groundwork for everything that is to happen in civic action projects. Jen Cody, Lori McGarry, and Liz Cullin, the Park Forest fifth-grade teachers, employ a number of powerful strategies to do this—ongoing "bucket-filling" for students to recognize each other's acts of kindness and support; "stepping over the line," in which they consider issues and experiences in their lives; and the classroom constitution by which they set expectations for working together and treating one another with respect. Teachers use many more rich and reflective activities to accomplish this. Here are a few (and there are still more in Chapter 7):

- **Appreciating learning styles.** One creative strategy used by a savvy biology teacher is the human graph of learning styles. Here's how it works:

  Step 1: Ask students to complete a short learning style inventory. (There are many online, but here are three: Learning Style Inventory by Brett Bixler at Pennsylvania State University, www.personal.psu.edu/bxb11/LSI/LSI.htm; Learning-Styles-Online.com, http://learning-styles-online.com; Multiple Intelligences Self-Assessment, at edutopia, www.edutopia.org/multiple-intelligences-assessment.)

Step 2: Have students form three or four lines according to their most prominent learning style as revealed by the survey—a human graph, so to speak. Typical may be auditory, visual, interpersonal, and mathematical styles. Students in each line then talk over their style with others in their line, comparing stories of how they study and learn things.

Step 3: Ask students to pair up with someone from one of the other lines. If one group is much larger than the others, there can be some threesomes, so everyone gets to talk with at least one person whose style differs from his or her own. Ask students to talk over in their pairs or threes the advantages and/or disadvantages of having a team made up of similar learners or a variety of styles. Get reports from the groups, and encourage discussion of the pros and cons. The concluding point: people may approach work differently, but each person has something to contribute, so we need to appreciate each other's strengths.

- **Discovering group dynamics.** Divide the group into small teams of three to six people. Each team receives a box of straws and a large handful of straight pins. The objective is for each team to build a tower using the pins and straws within a given time period. The towers are to be "judged" on their height, strength, and creativity. When teams are finished, ask each one to discuss the way individuals participated in their group. Did someone take a leadership role? Did someone propose ideas for how to build the tower? Perhaps one or two took over the physical work of pinning the straws together. If there were disagreements, how did they get settled? What the students will be exploring is the nature of group dynamics and the roles group members take. This can help students consider what makes an effective, cooperating group and the ways that individuals contribute. Should roles be assigned or rotated? How can everyone's voice get heard? This understanding will be important for the group's ongoing collaboration.

- **Peace circles.** Students sit in a circle and speak about the topic or issue, one at a time consecutively, as a "talking stick" is passed around. This process eliminates the back-and-forth that can otherwise turn a thoughtful discussion into a debate as each side talks past the other. The practice is simple, yet leads students to listen thoughtfully and brings out voices otherwise overpowered by more outspoken students. Plenty of early-grade teachers will recognize this practice as similar to the "morning meetings" they often use. You'll find a more detailed description of peace circles (sometimes called "talking circles") in the next chapter (Pranis and Boyes-Watson 2015).

Teaching for Discussion and Collaboration

It's important to develop discussion and collaboration norms and skills as a regular practice, rather than wait for a conflict to flare. Three outstanding resources for this: Nancy Steineke's *Reading and Writing Together: Collaborative Literacy in Action*, Smokey Daniels and Nancy Steineke's *Teaching the Social Skills of Academic Interaction*, and Randy and Katherine Bomer's *For a Better World: Reading and Writing for Social Action*. These texts outline a great collection of strategies and activities for building habits of respectful discussion and mutual support in a classroom where strong opinions are bound to emerge. Here are a few of their approaches (summarized for brevity) in two categories: (1) teaching students to work and talk constructively together and (2) organizing discussions to facilitate thoughtful exchange of ideas.

Teaching the Skills of Collaboration

For teaching students to work together effectively, one big step is identifying the skills that are part of productive, collaborative work (Steineke 2002, p. 56; Bomer and Bomer 2001, pp. 47–51):

- Quiet voices
- Forming groups quickly
- On-task behavior
- Praising
- Taking turns
- Encouraging participation
- Friendliness and support
- Asking questions
- Asking follow-up questions

- Summarizing
- Asking for help
- Giving help
- Checking for understanding
- Developing consensus
- Using connective language ("Could you explain more about . . .")
- Encouraging more students to talk

Nancy reminds us that these skills are not automatically acquired by either students or adults, so it takes time to teach and practice them, one at a time. Of course, it's best—in the spirit of everything this book aims to promote—to have students themselves brainstorm a list of such skills. They'll think of many, and you can always add missing essentials yourself. Here are a few suggestions from Nancy and from Randy and Katherine Bomer.

To help students see what's involved in each skill, Nancy uses T-charts with one column labeled "Looks Like" and the other, "Sounds Like." As a class, students fill in the chart for a particular skill, and this becomes a guide for the group.

To help students see and experience these skills in action, Randy and Katherine out-line several activities:

- **Fishbowl conversations.** Four or five students hold a conversation on a controversial topic while the rest of the class observes and takes notes. The observers—along with the "fish" in the middle—then share what they've observed and identify lessons all can learn about how to have a good conversation.

- **Recording or filming conversations.** Reading or hearing their own dis-cussion can help students see and reflect on how their discussions go—who talks more, how people do or don't listen to one another or respond to what another person is saying.

- **Responding to texts with different points of view.** Guiding students to think deeply about something they are reading not only gives them more to say, but also more ways to consider, analyze, and appreciate what other students are saying. One way to promote this is to introduce several related texts with differing points of view or kinds of information and ask students to compare them. Another is to introduce a social issue and invite students to examine a story they are reading through the lens of that issue. For ex-ample, the concept of imbalances in power between individuals provides a way to think about the teacher-student relationship in Sandra Cisneros' short story "Eleven".

(Bomer and Bomer 2001, pp. 46–48, 50–52)

You'll notice that all of the teachers featured in this book use a variety of these strate-gies. The Park Forest fifth-grade teachers help students learn to listen to and respect one another's point of view. Their students also compare various news sources on the same issue. Jean Klasovsky helps students listen to and support one another, especially through restorative justice peace circles. Polaris Academy and Prosser High School stu-dents learn how to find consensus and work collaboratively in small groups. Heather Van Benthuysen's students (as you will see in Chapter 7) learn to question thoughtfully, especially as they reflect on projects they have undertaken.

Organizing Discussions for Thoughtful Exchange of Ideas and Reaching Consensus

OK, so you're getting students accustomed to listening to one another, and contribut-ing constructively to a discussion. But because the work is, ideally, close to their hearts, class discussions can provoke passionate disagreement. Providing structures for helping to keep a conversation going respectfully and to ultimately reach consensus can help students not only to stay focused on their common goal, but also to handle difficult situations in their lives beyond the classroom. Here are a few great starting points:

- **Conversation partners.** Many teachers call this "turn and talk." It's perhaps the simplest and yet most effective tool for getting good discussion going. It just means taking a minute or two for everyone to talk with a partner about a particular question or issue before opening up to the whole class. It helps ensure that everyone has something to say and gets a chance to say it, at least with their partner (Bomer and Bomer 2001, pp. 48–49).

- **Writing as a thinking device.** Often called "quick write" or "stop and write." The teacher can ask everyone in the class or in a group to pause a discussion and jot notes for a couple of minutes about what they are thinking (as the Park Forest students are doing in Figure 5–1). Sharing some of these can bring out fresh ideas or voices that haven't been heard (Bomer and Bomer 2001, pp. 48–49).

- **Four corners.** In this book's introductory story, Elizabeth Robbins' students used this activity to try to settle on which of several issues to investigate. Students gather in separate corners of the room based on the stands they are taking. The four points may be "strongly agree," "somewhat agree," "somewhat disagree," and "strongly disagree." In Elizabeth's class the corners were the differing issues that various students wanted to address. Those in each corner talk over their position and their reasons for favoring

Figure 5–1 Writing Can Help Students Think Before Discussing

it. Each group then appoints a spokesperson who explains that group's stand. This may or may not lead to a solution, but it does help to surface the ideas and arguments each group has to share (Daniels and Steineke 2014, pp. 163–166).

- **Human continuum.** When there are two opposing points of view, students are invited to form a line, with those holding the strongest opinions on each side at the two ends of the line. Students who lean one way or the other, or who are ambivalent, find their appropriate places in line by comparing one another's thinking. Next, the line folds in half—that is, students who have differing points of view are now opposite one another. Pairs from the two sides explain their positions and, at the teacher's urging, listen attentively to one another. It's always interesting, after the discussions, to find out who may have changed their opinion about the issue (Daniels and Steineke 2014, pp. 158–162).

Time, Once Again

Obviously, building students' capacity to converse and listen empathically takes time, just when teachers are feeling more pressure to prepare for the ever-present standardized tests by which they are being judged. So it's important to understand and be able to explain to parents and administrators—and to yourself—why it's essential to provide both the training for good discussion and collaboration and the time to address difficult classroom issues when they come up. Here are some reasons to consider.

1. Foremost is our students' overall growth into thoughtful, responsible adults who can participate constructively in community efforts. Habits of listening with an open mind, empathizing with others, and actively contributing to deliberation are essential for a healthy community.
2. Participating in deep conversations on challenging issues develops students' critical thinking, which standards claim to promote.
3. Understanding and mutual support among students in a classroom mean fewer disruptions and thus actually more time on task.
4. When students feel heard by teachers and peers, they experience a greater sense of belonging in school—and more and more research on positive mindsets like belonging shows that they lead to higher academic achievement (Farrington et al. 2012).

Peer Conferencing

Especially with social action projects, you and the students will want their writing, presentations, and media to be as clear, thorough, and persuasive as possible. And since you're giving students as much responsibility as they can handle, critiquing one another's work will be important. You can teach students to do that in respectful and helpful ways. The first and most important step is for the giver of feedback to invite the writer or speaker to reflect on her own performance:

- How do you think you did?

- What parts do you feel best about?

- What parts do you want to improve?

- How might you do that?

- What help do you want from me?

It is most important for you to model critiquing. Students can learn from observing and experiencing conferences you conduct with them, to see how a thoughtful adult approaches this task. The objective is to show students how they can be helpful without being judgmental in either a harsh or overly complimentary way. You can demonstrate this in a fishbowl role-play. If another adult is available to play the part of the writer or speech author, that's great, but a confident student can easily take on the role. Ask students to jot notes on what they observe as you role-play, and share these to identify characteristics of thoughtful response and dialogue.

Next, using a gradual-release approach, have the whole class take the role of responders using the list of characteristics they've just made to guide them as you present a piece you have written. And finally, students can practice responding to each other's work in pairs. But especially if this approach is new, it may take a while to accustom students to it, so don't hesitate to repeat the guidelines when needed. Minilessons on particular writing or speech-making strategies can help add expertise to the conversations. Students can be amazingly perceptive about each other's work. You can help them exercise this ability in constructive ways.

CLASSROOM WORKSHOP

If open dialogue is the current that flows through a classroom, then writers' workshop provides a conduit for that energy. The concept of a workshop comes, as the name implies, not from school but from millennia of artists' and artisans' shops, where apprentices developed their skills under the guidance of an expert by creating products and art together. Classroom workshop-style instruction was originally developed for teaching writing, but just about any subject can be tackled this way. As you'll see, the key elements of classroom workshop fully support the social action projects explored in this book:

- Students work on tasks directly in class, either as individuals or in groups or teams. They do not listen to lectures, nor are they expected to magically produce work on their own after school. They work in the classroom, where they can benefit from the teacher's guidance and from the support other students can provide.

- Students exercise a considerable amount of choice about what to work on and how to approach tasks and challenges.

- The teacher may begin or intervene with a short minilesson or explanation to help students with a particular skill or strategy. This often involves modeling to show students how a competent adult handles the task.

- The other important role for the teacher is to consult with individuals or small groups to see how they are doing and provide help by asking questions strategically—but not to do the task for them.

- After a period of work, a few students share with the rest of the class what they have discovered, created, or accomplished. The class may respond simply by appreciating the work, critiquing it, or making further use of it, as appropriate.

- Students maintain portfolios or other records of their work for future use or further development, and for their own reflection and self-evaluation.

Workshop is not a curriculum or a program. It's simply a way to organize the classroom to enable student choice, simultaneous pursuit of a variety of tasks, and individualized help by teachers. So a typical workshop period in fifth grade at Park Forest School (described in Chapter 1) might look like this:

5 min.   Kids get out their folders and get organized to work for the period

10 min.   Minilesson on, for example, the elements of a CHIRP defense presentation

5 min.   Status-of-the-class round in which each student indicates briefly what he or she will work on during the period and whether help is needed

25 min.   Work time, during which students are writing or researching on whatever stage they're at, while the teacher circulates to hold brief conferences with students who request help

| 10 min. | Sharing time, when a few students volunteer to share what they've written so far and get feedback from the class; alternatively, the class as a whole reflects on how the work is going |
| 5 min. | Putting materials and folders away |

This classroom arrangement has been heavily used by teachers of English and writing across the grade levels, so there's plenty of help available. See the books listed under "Implementing Classroom Workshop" in the Resources section.

Why Workshop Structure Is Helpful for Teaching and Learning with Social Action

Workshop opens many possibilities for classroom activity that can't really be handled in a traditional whole-class setting:

1. It enables students to accomplish a variety of tasks on the spot.

2. It maximizes students' choices and initiative in a productive way.

3. The structure is flexible and can accommodate individual, small-group, and whole-class work.

4. The teacher can easily see if and how students are getting work done.

5. The teacher can discern what students need help with or where they are stuck on a problem and provide help immediately, rather than finding out too late that something impeded the work.

As Park Forest teacher Lori McGarry (one of the teachers whose classroom is described in Chapter 1) explains, the minilessons she regularly teaches within workshop enable students to build the writing skills they'll need. Separate minilessons focus on the various parts of their projects—the introductory "Dear Reader" piece, the informational section, the persuasive argument, and so on. And the differentiation in workshop enables students to work at their own pace. As her colleague, Jen Cody, emphasizes, writers' workshop encourages students to develop their own authentic voices and express their views on the topics they investigate.

The Teacher's Role

If you're new to workshop it can seem challenging, because so much control is released to the students, and so much goes on at once. A key objective is for students to take as much responsibility as they can possibly handle, and even to let some mistakes happen so kids figure out what works by themselves, rather than waiting for a teacher to tell them what to do. This can indeed feel risky, especially because we do not know in advance how a project will unfold. Teachers like Elizabeth Robbins (in the introduction) and Heather Van Benthuysen (in Chapter 7) tell us, however, that they are often surprised at the creative ideas students come up with, and are rarely disappointed with the results. We can have faith that the process will work. Still, there's plenty for the teacher to do. Your role is as essential as ever, and includes many steps:

- Explaining the workshop structure and helping students to create behavioral norms for it

- Prompting students to brainstorm, read, and/or survey to identify an issue or issues to investigate and to make a variety of decisions along the way

- Conducting minilessons on seeking root causes for issues, using research strategies, working together collaboratively in groups, resolving disagreements, asking good interview questions, approaching adults in positions of authority, using writing strategies for reports and persuasive letters, and more

- Holding conferences with individuals and groups to help them or to encourage them to solve problems

- Moving students from one stage to the next in their project(s)

- Observing to make sure students are working productively and collaboratively, and intervening to teach or reteach a strategy for working together if they are having difficulty

- Encouraging and supporting students when they encounter obstacles

- Assessing the learning that takes place

Following is a closer look at these workshop elements and teacher roles that may need attention to get them working well. Many aspects of workshop, such as student decisions about what to focus on, what to research, and what to write, are exactly the core elements of teaching and learning with social action described throughout this book.

Workshop Components

While every classroom workshop is unique, here is a bit more detail on the typical workshop components listed above. Once you get these established, you'll find that a workshop classroom flows quite smoothly, and students begin to demand more and more time to do the work that they become invested in.

Norms and Expectations

Some teachers worry that—kids being kids—independent or small-group work means time wasted and good order lost. So it's important to set norms for a workshop classroom and maintain them. The best way to do this—not surprisingly given our focus on student initiative—is to ask the class to do this together. Typically, students will generate a list similar to the following:

- Everyone should help and not leave it to just a few to do all the work.

- Everyone has strengths and talents, so we should find ways for each person to contribute.

- When we discuss an idea or decision, everyone should have a voice.

- If you disagree with someone about some part of the work, be sure to listen to him or her and explain your view respectfully.

- We should use our work time well. If you are finished with a task or don't know what to do next, talk to the teacher or another student to find something that will help the project.

Since students are not fully mature adults, it's natural that they may need reminding and review of these norms (of course, adults would *never* need such reminders!). This is simply a part of teaching and helping students to grow into collaborative and productive human beings. It also requires plenty of walking round the room and using the eyes in back of their heads that most teachers grow, to make sure everyone is making good use of the time.

Minilessons

Even as a teacher provides plenty of opportunity for students to make choices and carry out projects themselves, helping them acquire necessary skills remains essential. In a classroom workshop, this support is provided as the need arises through brief and timely minilessons. A classic approach that both helps and gives initiative to students is the *gradual release of responsibility*. These are the basic steps:

1. The teacher demonstrates the skill, using a projected image or other method that lets students see her work as she does it.

2. Students try it out together as a whole class.

3. They do another practice round of the work either as individuals or in small groups, with the teacher moving about the room, providing close support.

4. Students go ahead to use the skill on their own.

Many teachers know this as "I do it, we do it together, you do it yourself." A good variation, especially for projects in which we are giving students as much responsibility as possible, can be brainstorming by the class as the first step: "OK, people, how can we handle this task?" Then after suggestions from the students, the teacher can go ahead: "All right, let's try one of these ideas. I'll do it first while you watch, and we can see how it works out."

In a typical lesson for her fifth-grade students at Park Forest Elementary School, Liz Cullin helps students with web research by leading a minilesson on using alternative terms in a search. With the kids in the computer lab, she projects on a screen how various synonyms plugged into a Google search bring up different sources. And since each student is conducting his or her own inquiry, she then circulates to help individuals as they try the process themselves.

Designing good minilessons is an art. Jen Cody, also at Park Forest, teaches a minilesson on the purposes for writing an "about the author" piece, and the use of detail appropriate to those purposes. Since this isn't simply a "skill" but involves conceptualizing the task, the lesson is a bit more complex. As Jen reads aloud a short bio of author J. K. Rowling, the students create a T-chart with "Observations" on one side of the "T" and "Questions" on the other. After the reading, students share their observations and questions. Then she reads a second biography and the kids compare the two. This leads students to discuss why readers would want to know about the author. Some likely answers: to learn the author's intent in presenting his or her work, to understand the author's interests, and to gauge the author's credibility.

For independent application, Jen ask students to work in pairs to develop a list of questions each would like to have answered about his or her partner. These questions then help students to shape their "about the author" essays.

Status of the Class

This is one of the simplest and handiest of tools for ensuring that workshop goes well. As students are getting organized each day, ask them to report in just a sentence or two about what they will be doing for the period, either individually or by representatives of small groups if that's how they are working. Keep a chart or log to track their comments, and be prepared to head straight to any individuals or groups who appear to be struggling or uncertain of their direction. Or if everyone needs the same sort of help, it may be time for a fresh minilesson for the whole class. As students grow accustomed to this procedure, they will know to figure out their task for the day and be ready to briefly name it before you begin the status reports.

Individual and Small-Group Conferences

When students are struggling, it is hugely tempting to guide them with thorough advice for solving their problem. As members of one of the "helping" professions, teachers want to see students succeed. But the experienced teachers portrayed in this book have shown how important it is to hold back and let students take the lead as much as possible. So the first step in a conference is to get the student talking. Donald Graves, the father of much of the contemporary work on teaching writing, always wisely encouraged teachers to ask a few basic questions:

- What's the work about—what are you trying to say (or find out, or do)?

- Where are you in the work—in the middle? Finished with a draft?

- What help do you want from me?

    (Graves 1983, pp. 96–139)

Then, based on what you learn, you can ask further questions that help the student work through the problem:

- So who is this person at the public transportation authority that you are writing to?

- What do you think he probably thinks about the problem you are investigating?

- What kinds of arguments do you think might make him like your solution?

- How might you be able to find out more about that?

In other words, find out first what the student is trying to do and how much he or she knows about the task. This will help you understand where students are in the work, where they're hung up, what help may or may not be needed, and what further questions to ask. Follow-up questions then serve more as nudges or encouragements for students to devise their own solutions to the problem. And allow plenty of wait time for answers before concluding that more direct help or advice is needed.

Finally, a student or group may choose a solution that you suspect is not the most effective. In this case you need to make your best judgment call: Is it better to let them find out for themselves that their solution is problematic? Or should you steer them in a better direction so they don't flounder and grow discouraged?

Keeping Track of Everything

In a workshop classroom there's a lot going on—students might be debating (in groups or as a class) which issues to focus on, doing individual research, holding interviews with visiting experts, conducting and analyzing surveys, planning goals and action strategies, writing letters and reports, and preparing and critiquing presentations. To make this manageable, both teacher and students need to keep track of it all. Students need to be able to recall and reflect on all they've done and value it for their adult future. And the teacher needs to be able to confirm students' learning, make adjustments to improve projects in the future, and show accountability for students' progress.

It helps to have students keep logs, journals, and folders containing their work. One teacher learned this the hard way when she tried to walk her high school juniors back through the weeks of effort on a project without any written record and drew lots of blank looks. Young people live mainly in the present, at least consciously. A large chart on the wall or a class digital spreadsheet kept by a student secretary can help everyone track progress and recall past successes and struggles. Student folders can hold artifacts, notes, and logs that record steps the class has taken and contributions each student has made. You can easily create your own forms to copy and circulate, to help kids organize all this information.

If you're concerned about meeting particular standards, you and the students can keep a list and check them off along with the date(s) as things get done. Finally, it's a good idea to pause and reflect with the class every so often about what has been accomplished and where they are headed next.

ASSESSMENT

So you have lots of information—but how do you assess its value and significance? This is the necessity teachers always wrestle with, right? Assessment is especially important to consider in regard to student empowerment since it's at the core of the power relationship between students and teachers. Further, true accountability involves informing the community about the impact of the work they are paying for—which does not actually require "grading" each student. Yet, in the present era, with a business-style focus on a constant flow of data (whether it actually reflects or enables real learning or not), testing every student has become a constant intrusion on instruction. What educators really need, instead, is information on students' learning that is

- reflective of actual learning of material, concepts, skills, and processes *that matter*

- useful for students and teachers to help them continually improve, and useful for parents and community as meaningful accountability measures

- promptly available

- as unobtrusive as possible (unless you are using performance assessments that lead to a special-occasion event) and as connected to teaching and learning as possible

That shouldn't be too hard!

What Can You Assess Meaningfully?

English teacher Heather Van Benthuysen places great emphasis on student reflection as a means of assessment. Before a project even begins, she asks students to brainstorm a set of civic skills and dispositions (see Chapter 7 for an example of these). Students consider, for example "How well did we collaborate? How did we listen to one another and respect differences of opinion? In what ways did we try to involve ourselves in community concerns?" Even if efforts to enact the skills aren't always perfect, reflections that acknowledge challenges and address how to do better represent "success" for Heather. And if a student isn't yet gaining such perspective, it's an occasion for discussing it with him or her, rather than just stamping a low grade on the writing.

As for assessing specifics of the work: there are abilities and chunks of knowledge in your subject area that you want to know students are learning, and that may be required by your district or by wider standards. You already know about these. But in addition, experts have identified student mindsets and abilities that are especially important for young people if they are to become empowered contributors to their community—which is what social action projects are about:

> *Agency*—acting or exerting influence and power in a given situation
>
> *Belonging*—developing meaningful relationships with other students and adults and having a role in the classroom and at the school
>
> *Competence*—developing new abilities
>
> *Discourse*—exchanging diverse ideas and opinions to work toward a common goal
>
> *Efficacy*—believing that one can make a difference in the world—and that one has a responsibility to do so
>
> (Based on Mitra and Serriere 2012, p. 743)

Increasingly, attitudes like a sense of belonging are being recognized as important factors in student achievement and success, so they are not just "touchy-feely." Farrington et al. (2013) review the growing research on this important aspect of learning in their book, *Teaching Adolescents to Become Learners: The Role of Noncognitive Factors in Shaping School Performance*. These attitudes can be measured in a variety of ways that good teachers have used—rubrics co-created with students, for example, or tracked, using carefully designed questionnaires. The National Action Civics Collaborative provides an extensive questionnaire on its website (see the Standard Action Civics Student Post-Survey on the Action Civics Evaluation tab of http://actioncivicscollaborative.org/resources/toolbox/) for students to reflect on the value of their project work and its effect on their present and future civic involvement. Numerous questions focus on aspects of agency, collaborative discourse, and efficacy.

More open-ended student reflection is just as helpful, especially if it's structured by five or six key questions that you want them to think about. Mikva Challenge uses the following set of questions that focus especially on the action end of a project:

1. Were we successful in achieving our goal(s)? How do we know? What evidence do we have that our ideas will be, or were, put into effect?

2. What worked with the action(s) we took? What was successful?

3. What could have been improved upon? How could we have made our action more effective?

4. Did we make a good choice in our goal? Our strategy? Could we have chosen a different action to take? Why?

5. How did I personally contribute to the project? What part of my contribution am I most proud of?

6. What have I learned about the ability of everyday people to create change? Is it possible? What are the most important reasons why some people succeed and others don't?

7. What have I learned about my own power (think about your skills, knowledge, and attitudes as a result of talking this class—how have they changed)?

(Mikva Challenge 2015, pp. 257–258)

While it wouldn't be appropriate to downgrade students who don't have positive answers to some of the questions, it's important for students and teachers, as well as parents and community members, to know whether the students' work has resulted in a change of mindset about responsible civic action, and how to make improvements if that didn't happen—which is what real accountability is about.

Students Can Help Plan Assessment

How assessment will work depends on whether projects are done individually, in small groups, or by the whole class together. But rather than provide a neat, predesigned rubric for specific products that are part of the work, the best path is to create it by a class brainstorm. If your students are excited about the project and have a sense of what is coming (as the Park Forest fifth graders in Chapter 1 did because of the reputation of the projects in the school), you may opt to do this near the start. If your students are less confident, you may decide to wait until they've chosen an issue and their research has begun to generate engagement, so kids are not overwhelmed by the prospect of the work ahead. Some steps in this process:

1. Share some artifacts from a typical project at the grade level you are teaching. These could be letters to government officials, presentation scripts students used to inform community groups, student-created informational videos—or even a product like a curriculum unit for teachers to use. Students can review these items and discuss their strengths and limitations. If this is the first time you are conducting a social action project, you may need to find some examples online. Videos and materials from a number of projects can be seen on the website of What Kids Can Do (www.whatkidscando.org/specialcollections/student_research _action/index.html). Good examples include "Deaf Students Teach Restaurants to Serve with Respect" and "Denver Teenagers Take Action for Social Change."

2. Based on this material, invite students to brainstorm elements of the work that they deem especially important.

3. If this was a group project, ask students to list ways they think the project creators contributed and collaborated to get it done.

4. Guide the class to narrow their list of characteristics and combine related ones until they arrive at a manageable set of the most important items.

If projects are done individually, the list will apply separately for each student. If the effort is organized by small groups or the whole class, it's best to still assess each individual student's contribution. Student logs and your own status of the class charts will be useful for identifying the particular work each student did. Smart teachers have learned that a low group grade can create resentment and problems with classroom climate if some students blame fellow group members for a poor mark.

The final list you end up with essentially provides a rubric that you and the students can use, not only to evaluate work at the end of a project, but also to guide students in both their process and content as the effort proceeds. And as Heather Van Benthuysen asserts, students' reflection on how they did and what they learned is as important as the product itself.

Performance Assessment

Projects with social action offer a perfect opportunity for presentations and other types of performance—including videos, Prezis, dramatic skits, and more. Performance assessment does take time and organizing, but if the performances actually help advance the change that students seek, they could form a valuable part of the project itself—for once, assessment becomes a part of learning and doing rather than an afterthought. Some elements to plan for:

- If the projects are done individually you'll have a large number of presentations to schedule. A solution is to have three or four presentations take place simultaneously, with the rest of the class or a wider audience divided up to view them. You'll need help from additional adults to guide the various groups.

- If students are working in small groups or as a whole class, you'll want them to make sure each person gets a turn to explain or enact some aspect of the project. The last thing you want is for just one or two go-getter performers to do all the talking.

- Having a larger audience besides just fellow students seems especially desirable considering the community dimension of the work. This is a great way to showcase your project and students' learning for parents and other community members. And it makes the presentations especially meaningful, giving students the role of educating adults (and/or other students) about their issue. Including a wider audience of course adds other tasks— creating and distributing invitations, making sure people actually come so that students are not disappointed, preparing a program or other orientation for audience members, and so on. Put the kids to work on this rather than trying to do it all yourself.

- If explicit assessment is involved, you'll want to decide whether all audience members contribute or just a few appointed judges (or let's call them feedback providers).

- The performances are the mode by which students share what they've learned. But you'll still need a rubric or guide to identify elements of learning displayed in the performances that you and the students consider most important. This can be used by you, of course, but also by the students (both as audience members and for self-assessment) or by parents and other guests.

- Students will need rehearsal time—unless they are simply showing a video or other electronic product.

This approach may take a lot of planning and work, but it's bound to be memorable for the kids and highly informative for the larger audience, whether that includes just other students in the school, the faculty, or the wider community.

HANDLING DIFFICULT MOMENTS

So you've provided all this wonderful skill building and you've overseen lots of deep and probing conversations. But then a child blurts out a really insensitive or biased remark, just as a student in Katherine Bomer's classroom once did, declaring, "Sherrisa [another student in the class] can't be president of the United States." Not knowing whether this remark was about race or gender, Katherine neither ignored the comment nor contradicted nor lectured about it, but brought the class together for a discussion. She began by asking the student to explain more about what he meant. This in turn led to a mini-inquiry by the class on women's goals and desires for their lives, followed by frequent follow-up reports on the topic as students encountered related evidence during the year (Bomer and Bomer 2001, p. 45).

Randy and Katherine Bomer also describe a class in which one student persisted in voicing strongly racist beliefs and complaining about reading books on black and Native American experience. Katherine left it to the rest of the students to disagree with him, and while the boy never relented, she was convinced that letting the class debate the issue was the healthiest approach, enacting a democratic classroom rather than silencing his voice or theirs (Bomer and Bomer 2001, pp. 109–110).

Elizabeth Robbins (featured in the introduction) explains a number of steps she takes when such moments occur—as they almost always do, she says, when big social issues are involved.

- Stress from the beginning of the year that we're all responsible for keeping the classroom a safe place where everyone is respected. Point out, too, that the class may need to have some hard discussions, since some issues can be contentious. If a student raises controversial issues or beliefs, he or she can expect that others may voice disagreement.

- When a judgmental or discriminatory remark is made, the teacher can stop the discussion and ask that students do some research for evidence about the situation or group that has been denigrated. Elizabeth stresses that it helps to put a human face on the people being labeled. Twitter feeds, videos, and written accounts of people's struggles help give students a fuller perspective on others' lives. Personal stories are a powerful learning tool.

This work of deepening students' understanding of other cultures and points of view takes time—but after all, it means more learning and exercising academic skills—researching, sifting evidence, writing, speaking, and debating thoughtfully. Not to mention learning respect, openness, and civil discourse.

When a complex project is done as a group, students' differences may be more about particular steps to take, division of responsibilities, or other aspects of a group's dynamics. This is when all the work you've done to help students set norms, practice constructive discussion, and support and appreciate one another pays off. Students may find they need to add particular norms to their list for taking turns, compromising, or making sure everyone has a say. An occasional peace circle may help resolve an issue. And it's a good idea to regularly hold team-building and class culture activities (see Chapters 1 and 7) rather than using them just to get acquainted at the start of the year.

Interactions within groups of human beings are always complex in dozens of big and small ways, and you'll find yourself problem solving as you go. Nancy Steineke, an expert at explaining the many twists and strategies for managing a classroom full of strong egos, suggests that even details that might seem minor can make a big difference—such as arranging the room so students don't go wandering unnecessarily, optimizing group size, and giving positive group recognition rather than the group grades that can create more conflict than incentive (Steineke 2002, pp. 94–110).

The Park Forest fifth-grade teachers find that the community-building work they do from the start of the year goes a long way toward ensuring that students not only get along and work well together, but help to right the classroom ship when currents get rough. Jen Cody recounts one occasion when students decided to learn about each other's religions. One student began blurting out insensitive questions, including, "Don't you people worship cows?" Before Jen had a chance to intervene, a girl sitting next to the questioner quietly and gently reined him in, whispering, "That's really not appropriate." Teachers don't always get to witness the deep growth that can take place as we work with our students. But when we do, it confirms all the effort we put into making our classrooms safe and productive spaces.

SOCIAL ACTION IN THE SCHOOL THROUGH RESTORATIVE JUSTICE

In this book, we've considered inquiry and action within a school as well as in the larger community. However, we have not yet discussed action that takes aim at serious injustices in the culture of a school itself. It certainly could seem contradictory if students were to take on meaningful and complex issues in the larger world while neglecting them right at home. And one of the biggest issues in many schools is student discipline. Particularly in urban schools, it has worked for too long like this: student disrupts class so teacher sends him (more often it is indeed "him") to the discipline office or dean, where he receives a five- or ten-day suspension. Late to class? Same punishment. Rowdy at lunch? Ditto. Arrive at school not in proper uniform? You guessed it.

With federal recognition that this practice has been discriminatory, the process is beginning to change, but discipline remains a thorny issue in many schools. After a ten-year study of school disciplinary policies, a task force of the American Psychological Association found that zero-tolerance polices not only do not improve school safety; they likely make schools *less* safe (Restorative Practices Working Group 2014). Instead of seeing school as a community, students in zero-tolerance environments often feel frustrated, humiliated, embarrassed, resentful, and disconnected. Extreme and automatic policies such as suspending students for minor infractions deny kids valuable learning time, discourage trusting student-teacher relationships, and encourage—or even force—students to leave school permanently before graduating. As high school history teacher Jean Klasovsky puts it: "The punishment for missing class is . . . missing more class." This is not just the story of a few isolated students: the negative effects of punitive policies are widespread and systematic, funneling marginalized students (most often minority students and students with disabilities) into the school-to-prison pipeline.

Restorative justice—strategies to repair harm caused by or revealed by disruptive behavior—provides an effective alternative to these disciplinary practices. And as we shall see, the work is the responsibility of students who have received training—so it is a form of social action that students can effectively implement in their own schools. It does not follow the choice-research-plan-and-act cycle of other projects described in this book, but it complements them, operating in the same sphere of student voice and responsibility.

RESTORATIVE JUSTICE IN ACTION: A PEER COUNCIL AT REILLY SCHOOL

Walking into Room 310, the Peace Room at Reilly School, the first things you see are two recycled but still plushy couches and a large easy chair, arranged in a U around a blue living room carpet. Cans of calm pastel paints sit atop old school cabinets, left over from a volunteer redecorating job. High up across from the door are colored sheets with peer council members' names and welcoming declarations—"We listen to your problems." "We're here for you." Below these hangs a large erasable calendar listing the month's council activities.

The peer council (or, as many schools call it, a "peer jury") meets in the Peace Room Fridays after school with students referred by the dean for all but the most serious disciplinary issues. The focus of this process is to restore the social fabric of the community so that all, including the student in trouble, can feel safe and accepted.

On a Friday just before spring break, the council was eager to get to work, even though vacation week would begin the moment they were finished. Four eighth-grade council members took on the case of a fifth-grade boy who had been referred for a physical action toward another student (details are confidential—an essential principle of the process). The mood among the council members was serious yet caring. The younger boy, just about trembling with anxiety, knew he would be referred back to traditional disciplinary action if he did not work with the peer council—and he was facing a group of the oldest and most responsible students in the school. The lead juror began by introducing the council members and passing around a confidentiality oath for all to sign. The team's questions then followed a classic progression:

- What exactly took place that got the student in trouble?

- What motivated the student to act in this unacceptable way?

- How did the student feel about the situation?

- How did the student think others in the room felt?

- What would it be like if the student were in the other person's shoes?

- What would the student do next time a situation of this sort were to come up?

- What could be some possible solutions to help make up for what happened?

Then council members worked with the fifth grader to write a contract—steps he agreed to take to repair the damaged relationships. The mood of the entire process was serious, but not focused on punishment. As one team member explained optimistically at the end of their time together, "We want you to feel refreshed."

You might wonder if this kind of personalized, student-driven system is, perhaps, taking place in a tiny boutique school, or if the community that the school serves is some sort of privileged oasis. In fact, Reilly has over a thousand students, and 95 percent of its families are at low income levels. The restorative justice work in the school is the culmination of a long-term effort by the school's art teacher, Mauricio Pineda, who also teaches classes in DePaul University's Peace, Justice, and Conflict Studies program. As a result, Reilly now includes both a peer council (see the team at work in Figure 6–1) and a Peace Room, where students can come to cool down and get support when they are stressed, along with a growing use of "peace circles" to build the social and learning climate in classrooms.

Figure 6–1 The Reilly School Peer Council Team at Work

WHAT IS RESTORATIVE JUSTICE?

We can trace restorative justice back to the First Nation indigenous peoples of North America. In her article, "Restorative Justice Practices of Native American, First Nation and Other Indigenous People of North America," Laura Mirsky (2004) quotes Robert Yazzie, Chief Justice Emeritus of the Navajo Nation Supreme Court:

> *The first order of business the relatives would do in the peacemaking process is to get to the bottom of a problem. In court, I would sue you for battery and the state would say we have to prove all the elements of a crime and use the rules or the law to prove that you are guilty. The Holy People say that's beside the point. What matters here is: why did this act happen in the first place? There's a reason why the harm has occurred. Let's deal with that. Maybe we have a history of problems between the two of us. If we can get to the bottom of a problem, all the other stuff will fall into place. The damage can be acknowledged by you, and I can go away happy from the process, knowing that you say that you're not going to do it again.*

In the same article, Judge Joseph Flies-Away echoes the benefits of constructive handling of civil disturbances rather than the more punitive European tradition our country follows, explaining that someone who commits a crime "acts like he has no relatives. People do the worst things when they have no ties to people. Tribal court systems are a tool to make people connected again."

Today, restorative justice draws on this tradition. As the coalition FixSchoolDiscipline.org explains, "Restorative Justice invites a fundamental shift in the way we think about and do justice, from punishing individuals after wrongdoing to repairing harm and preventing its reoccurrence" (Fix School Discipline 2015).

In the vignette above, the peer council worked with the younger boy to help him reflect and bring resolution—not vengeance or punishment—to the school community. This enables the student who has misbehaved to take responsibility and return to and even strengthen the classroom, rather than being further removed from it. As Ted Wachtel, president of the International Institute for Restorative Practices, explains, restorative justice can "prevent conflict and wrongdoing" by "proactively build[ing] relationships and a sense of community" (Wachtel 2013). Research compiled by the institute reveals that in three sample schools where restorative practices were introduced, serious behavioral infractions and suspensions declined by 60 percent or more. Another study

Academic Benefits of Restorative Justice

Both restorative justice and other kinds of learning with social action ask students to develop particular knowledge, social skills, and mindsets. Many of these echo items in the Common Core standards, particularly the skills of inquiring closely into a narrative, gathering and evaluating evidence, and exchanging ideas effectively as a group. For peer council sessions, these skills include:

- Interviewing and questioning to gain understanding of a problem. It is especially important in peer council to ask pertinent follow-up questions to learn the events surrounding a situation and to understand the referred student's motivations.
- Developing rapport with a person who may be feeling defensive. This requires maintaining a nonjudgmental and even empathic stance while acknowledging that a wrong may have been committed.
- Actively listening to make sure to understand what's being said.
- Evaluating statements to determine their accuracy or trustworthiness.
- Brainstorming solutions to issues.
- Working collaboratively and sharing the effort as a team.
- Building a sense of responsibility for the community, whether that is the school, the neighborhood, or the city where the student lives.

For an excellent overview of restorative justice and its effects in a school, view the TEDx talk by history teacher Jean Klasovsky, who for four years oversaw the program at Farragut Career Academy High School in Chicago: www.youtube.com/watch?v=tqktOiYG5NM

showed that restorative justice in a school sharply narrowed the racial gap in misconduct referrals (International Institute for Restorative Practices 2014). Jean Klasovsky outlines additional academic benefits in her TEDx talk that can be viewed on YouTube.

LAYING THE GROUNDWORK FOR RESTORATIVE JUSTICE IN YOUR SCHOOL

A first step is to build understanding and support for your effort, since much of the activity of restorative justice connects with the whole school and not just your individual classroom. Give yourself time to get it done. One key to making this happen is one-on-one conversations. This is one of the most effective tools for promoting change in a community or organization. As any community organizer will tell you, one-on-ones, as they like to call them, are their stock-in-trade.

Here are some ground rules for conducting one-on-ones:

- **Be mindful of others' time.** A one-on-one is a conversation in which you aim primarily to build a basis of understanding and trust with another person. A good one-on-one will take half an hour or so—long enough to have a discussion of some depth, but not demanding too much time from the other person's schedule. Since your principal is likely very busy and overscheduled, your talk with him or her may well be much shorter.

- **Listen and respond.** In a one-on-one you're learning about a person, not trying to move your agenda. If you approach the session with the same kind of openness and interest that you might show a trusted colleague, the conversation is more likely to benefit both of you. Learn about that person's interests and values and share your own. Ask questions like, "How did you get into teaching in the first place?" And, "So what are some things that are especially important to you in working with students?" Respond with examples and stories of your own. The discussion is give-and-take, not an interview. It's OK to ask probing questions to better understand your partner's thinking, but you are not trying to convert him or her to your point of view.

- **Don't look for an immediate payoff.** You aren't seeking explicit help or commitment from your discussion partner at this point unless he or she volunteers it.

- **Hold one-on-ones with lots of colleagues.** Obviously you'll need to talk with the principal, but plan to sit down with other influential colleagues as well. The disciplinary dean, if your school has one, will be essential. You may have a few favorite colleagues who can be of help to start with, and there are probably several influential teachers everyone looks up to. Approaching doubters can be important as well. If you are starting a peer council, you'll want colleagues to make good use of it. You'll find more help for one-on-ones in Chapter 8.

IMPLEMENTING RESTORATIVE JUSTICE IN YOUR SCHOOL

There are five key elements of restorative justice: peer councils, peer mediation, peace circles, care rooms, and conflict resolution. The following practical strategies will help you to make these into realities for your students' school experience. No matter which elements you choose to start with, the most important stakeholders in a school building are the students.

Implementing a Peer Council

A peer council may be the easiest part of restorative justice to start with because it doesn't require a deep change in classroom management style on the part of faculty, and students very readily embrace the concept and sign on as members. Peer councils meet with an offending student (and sometimes the victim) to understand what happened and work out an agreed-upon process of repair and reconciliation, as shown in the earlier example from Reilly School. Some schools refer to this group as a "peer jury." Here's how four seventh- and eighth-grade peer council members at Reilly School view the work they have done together:

> **Carolina:** *If you're referred, you're getting help. Someone is there to support you. And there's always a story behind what happened that explains it.*

> **Maria:** *Being a council member makes you a better person. It makes you think about another person's point of view. It relaxes me—because I'm helping someone out but not being forced to do it.*

Brayan: *It helps keep me on track and stay focused. I enjoy peer council, so I need to stay out of trouble.*

America: *To be a good council member you need to have a lot of patience. You can get frustrated when the person doesn't want to talk.*

Carolina: *You need to have confidence in yourself and believe you can help. You need to trust the person [who is in trouble]. And you need to keep to confidentiality.*

Brayan: *Peer council has helped the teachers too. They have less paperwork and kids have fewer problems, so they can do their teaching.*

Maria: *Before, we had lots of students in trouble and we could tell that the dean was stressed. Now her job is easier because she handles just the bigger cases.*

Probing deeply into an issue and analyzing its causes, taking responsibility, seeing empathically from other perspectives, gaining self-confidence, valuing self-growth, and making a difference for the school. What teacher wouldn't be proud to have her students doing all that?

Basic Peer Council Approach

Peer councils consist of groups of students (as few as three or as many as ten) neutrally helping a peer to resolve a conflict or make amends for some way he or she has disrupted the school or classroom community. They do not decide on consequences but rather help the referred student repair the social fabric. The student is asked to explain what took place and why, encouraged to consider how others felt about the situation, and invited to propose a solution. Council members are trained to get at the root of the problem, rather than simply identify the wrong committed. They learn to establish rapport, to listen respectfully, and to take a broader view than just the incident itself. They may make suggestions to help the student better integrate into the life of the school. A lead council member follows up to make sure the agreed-upon action is carried out.

Farragut Career Academy High School is another of the Chicago schools using a peer council. Farragut's "Restorative Practices Handbook" lays out three guiding principles:

1. Justice requires that we work to heal victims, offenders, and communities that have been injured.

2. Victims, offenders, and communities should have the opportunity for active involvement in the justice process.

3. The entire community is responsible for establishing and encouraging peace.

(Klasovsky et al. 2010)

Recruiting Students for Peer Council

When a council reflects the broad makeup of the school population, students who receive hearings can relate to the team members. The team should not be composed only of high achievers or those who participate in many school activities. Often, students who have been in trouble make the best council members because they can both empathize with referred students and imagine ways to reintegrate them into the school community. As a restorative justice leader you can seek student team members in a number of ways:

- Contact students you believe will be effective and empathetic council members and invite them to apply.

- Seek recommendations from teachers and counselors.

- Issue a school-wide invitation for student applications.

Sample recommendation and application forms are provided in Figures 6–2 and 6–3. According to guidelines from Alternatives, Inc., the organization that provides much of the restorative justice training in Chicago, good council members are those who can:

- Be compassionate, sincere, and respectful of participants.

- Let people vent their emotions.

- Stay neutral, while disapproving of the harm done. Jurors must not judge a person before listening to their situation. Jurors can demonstrate disapproval for the harm done and acknowledge what is owed to the person harmed.

- Try to *encourage* and *assist* the referred student to come up with his or her own solutions to repairing the harm instead of just telling them what to do. (Alternatives, Inc., "Restorative Peer Juries," p. B4)

As the peer council advisor, you have particular responsibilities as well:

- **Model the restorative behavior** you want to see in the council members—empathy, nonjudgmental, active listening, etc.

- **Build relationships**—take time to listen to students' concerns and get to know them.

- **Promote the program within the school** to increase staff buy-in.

- **Create a safe atmosphere**—be a friendly presence; prepare jurors and referred students.

Figure 6–2 Farragut Career Academy Peer Jury Recommendation Form

---

PEER JUROR RECOMMENDATION FORM

Name of student: _____ Home phone # _____

Name of person recommending peer juror: _____

School/Organization _____ Title: _____

I recommend _____ to be trained as a peer juror.

S/he possesses the following qualities which are important as a peer juror. (Please check those that apply and feel free to add others.)

_____ Respect

_____ Responsibility

_____ Concern for others

_____ Communication skills

_____ Sense of fairness

_____ Empathy

_____ Commitment

_____ Confidentiality

_____ Open-mindedness

_____ Other _____

I am recommending this student because:

Signature of reference person: _____

Date _____

Alternatives, Inc., "Restorative Peer Juries," p. B6.

May be photocopied for classroom use. *From Inquiry to Action* by Steven Zemelman. ©2016 (Portsmouth, NH: Heinemann).

Figure 6–3 Farragut Career Academy Peer
Jury Student Application Form

PEER JUROR MEMBERSHIP APPLICATION

**Applications are due at the end of the day on _____,
and should be turned in to _____ or the folder at
the counseling office.**

Name: _____ Advisor: _____

Address: _____

Zip code: _____ Home Phone: _____

Please circle: Freshman   Sophomore   Junior   Senior

Please circle: Male   Female

Peer jury meets: (day) _____ at (time) _____

Are you available during this time for meetings? (Circle one)

　YES　　NO

Why are you interested in becoming a peer juror?

_____

_____

_____

How could being a peer juror help you now and/or in the future?

_____

_____

_____

continues

What does "community" mean to you?

_____

_____

_____

Please describe what you believe would be the ideal school
community/climate.

_____

_____

_____

If you could change one thing about the school, what would it be
(please do not say "changing classes or teachers") and why?

_____

_____

_____

What do you think are the top three reasons that students act out in
class or get in fights in the school building?

_____

_____

_____

How do you think these issues should be handled?

_____

_____

_____

Training the Student Team

Agencies and school districts in many areas provide training for new student teams. In Chicago, the school district offers a full day of training several times per year sponsored by its Office of Social Emotional Learning and led by Alternatives, Inc. If such a resource is not available, you may need to obtain training for yourself during the summer and then serve as the trainer for your team—which can be great fun and rewarding in itself. At Farragut, advisors supplement district training with sessions on particular skills such as asking good follow-up questions, focusing on feelings, and wording questions in a nonaccusatory way, fitting these in on meeting days when no students were referred.

Young people like those at Reilly School are enthusiastic and impatient to get their peer council started. So it's a good idea to conduct short exercises on these approaches, followed by mock sessions to try them out. Team members are usually all too savvy at taking the role of the student in trouble, so the practice sessions can be surprisingly realistic, challenging, and often really hilarious.

Organizing and Conducting Sessions

First, there's scheduling to think about. Considering how tight school schedules can be, this takes some strategizing. Reilly School's council meets Fridays after school. When more than one case comes up, the team divides into subgroups to handle both simultaneously. At Farragut, where active students are always busy after school, the four teams—one for each grade level—each meet once a week during that grade's lunch period. Many high schools have weekly advisory periods that can be used if they're long enough and if this doesn't conflict with other important activities.

Referral process. You'll need a means for referring students who have caused a problem. In some schools these come directly from teachers to the council advisor, while in others a disciplinary dean will be the conduit. Guidelines for referral will depend on the school district's discipline code. Usually, outright violent actions are not eligible for peer council resolution.

Preparation. It's helpful to prepare the team before a hearing begins by reviewing the circumstances of the referral—though it's obviously important not to influence members' perspectives on the case. The referred student should be prepared as well. In a large school, the student may not be clear about the role of the council or the necessity of committing to a written agreement. Coming to peer council is voluntary, and if the student is not willing to reach an agreement he or she will be referred back to the standard school discipline process.

Key forms. At Farragut, team members and the referred student all sign a confidentiality agreement to highlight the importance of this aspect of the process. An agreement contract records in writing the actions that the student will take to repair the harm that has been done. Samples of these forms are provided in Figures 6–4 and 6–5.

Figure 6–4 Farragut Career Academy Peer
Jury Confidentiality Agreement

OATH OF CONFIDENTIALITY

**I promise as a peer juror/referred student/witness to not
share by written, spoken, or sign language any information
that is shared with me during a peer jury hearing.**

_____

Signature of Referred Student

Date _____

_____

Signature of Juror   Signature of Juror

_____

Signature of Juror   Signature of Juror

_____

Signature of Juror   Signature of Juror

_____

Signature of Adult Observer

Alternatives, Inc.

May be photocopied for classroom use. _From Inquiry to Action_ by Steven Zemelman. ©2016
(Portsmouth, NH: Heinemann).

Figure 6–5 Farragut Career Academy Peer
Jury Agreement Contract

PEER JURY AGREEMENT CONTRACT

Name of referred student _____

Date of hearing _____

Division _____ Division teacher _____

Action(s) agreed to by student to repair harm from reported incident:

_____

_____

_____

Agreed date for completion of action(s) _____

Follow-up to be completed by (peer juror) _____

on the following date _____

I (referred student), _____, understand that
if I satisfactorily complete this agreement, this matter will be closed
and my action(s) to repair the harm will be noted in my record. However, if I fail to complete this agreement, my case will be returned to
the school discipline office for other possible disciplinary action as
determined by the school administration.

Signed by:

_____

Referred Student

_____

Lead Juror

_____

Peer Jury Advisor

Follow-up report:
Contract completed _____   Contract not completed _____

Figure 6–6 Farragut Career Academy Lead Juror Guide Sheet

LEAD JUROR RESPONSIBILITIES AND SCRIPT
Responsibilities:

- Introduce the peer jury session using the script below.
- Appoint a timekeeper to notify when 10 minutes are left, then 5 minutes and 2 minutes.
- *Encourage all jurors to participate in the discussion.*
- Follow up on fulfillment of the contract—or another juror can be appointed.

~~~~~~

Lead Juror Script:

- Hi, my name is _____, and I will introduce the peer jury session today.
- Before we begin, let's all introduce ourselves. As we go around the room, please say your name and answer the question we've drawn from the Question Box.
- (A juror chooses a question from the box and reads it aloud.)
- As peer jurors, we are here to help you find a solution to your problem. We are not here to judge.
- If you complete the contract that we will help you create, you will not be suspended, and this incident will not go on your record.
- We will ask you some questions about yourself, about the situation that brought you here, and how you can restore things to a better state.
- We encourage you to be open and honest, so we pledge that everything said here is confidential. Everything said in this room stays in this room. I will pass around the Oath of Confidentiality for everyone to sign.
- Now let's get started.

Typical shape of a session. The description of the Reilly School's peer council session gives a good overview of a productive session, but it's worth reviewing the steps here. While every situation is different, most are likely to follow this basic procedure:

- A lead councilor explains the process to the referred student.

- The session starts with a warm-up activity to break the ice and help the referred student get comfortable discussing his or her situation. The Farragut team uses a "question box" with interesting queries that someone pulls out and hands around for everyone to answer.

- The council inquires about what took place that led to the difficulty.

- Council members ask about the student's motives for his or her actions—and learn more broadly about the student's mindset toward school and the people involved.

- Members find out the student's feelings about the situation—often the student is angry or feels disrespected or ashamed as a result of the events, and needs to get past that.

- Members help the student think about how others may have felt, and to imagine what it would be like to be in the other person's shoes.

- The student is encouraged to consider alternative actions or responses if a situation of the same sort were to come up again.

- The student and council together determine possible solutions the student can agree to, draw up a contract, and arrange for follow-up to confirm that the solution was carried out.

Role of the advisor. Ideally, the advisor is there mainly to provide a responsible adult presence. The conduct of the session is the council members' job. However, teacher-advisors find that they occasionally need to help the discussion along if a referred student is uncommunicative or the case is particularly challenging. The advisors too, after all, are part of the community. Of course, learning goes the other way as well, when thoughtful students make perceptive observations. Advisors have watched admiringly as skillful team members have told about their own similar struggles, gaining the trust of a hesitant student.

Implementing Peer Mediation

Peer mediation involves a small team of students (usually a pair) helping two or more peers to resolve a conflict. The mediators do not assume anyone was at fault but instead guide the adversaries to reach an understanding with one another. Thus the mediators must learn to maintain a stance of strict neutrality, compared with the assumption in councils that a referred student is involved in some sort of problem. Peer councils often meet with single students who are referred to them, while peer mediators usually meet with a pair of students who have come into conflict. A full peer mediation team may consist of a number of pairs that take turns leading mediations. The larger mediator team then meets regularly to further their training and discuss mediation strategies they've used.

Training for mediators and council members is similar. Both learn active listening skills, good questioning strategies, and ways to maintain confidentiality and establish trust with the students they are to help. Both discuss with their referred peers how to ensure that their problem does not recur. Council members, however, sometimes make suggestions about how to repair the harm that a student has caused, while mediators are careful to have referred students be the ones to decide on an agreement and resolve their issue.

Good online resources for peer mediation include:

- Study Guides and Strategies, Cooperative Learning Series, "Peer Mediation," www.studygs.net/peermed.htm
- School Mediation Associates, "Quick Guide to Implementing a Peer Mediation Program," www.schoolmediation.com/pdf/Quick-Guide-to-Implementing-a -Peer-Mediation-Program.pdf

---

Implementing Peace Circles

Now we turn to a restorative justice strategy usually guided by teachers rather than students. It's included here because it creates a climate of respect and mutual support and asks students to participate in creating that climate. Plus, it's a tool that can often be used in a class working on a social action project to address issues that come up within the class.

In a peace circle, participants sit in a circle and a "talking piece" is passed around to signal each person's turn to speak. No one is permitted to interrupt a speaker. This structure exerts a strong influence, especially when emotions are intense. Everyone gets heard, and people tend to listen well since their turn to speak is assured. The consecutive passing of the talking piece rather than a back-and-forth debate helps to mediate disagreements and ensures that many points of view get shared. A circle keeper—usually a teacher or counselor in the building—begins the process by setting the tone and the goals for the circle. An excellent document defining and outlining peace circle processes is available from Project Nia: www.project-nia.org/docs/Peacemaking _Circles_overview.pdf.

Jean Klasovsky, the high school history teacher whose talk on restorative justice we referred to earlier in this chapter, tells of the power of a peace circle she held to address racial tensions in her classroom one year:

> At the end of the conversation I asked the students, "What do we need to do to try to solve some of these problems? How should we address them?" Their response: We need to have more discussions like this one! After that day, the tension in that classroom started to melt away. I saw what an effect our circle had had when two students, one Black, one Mexican, chose to work together on a project, even though they had terrible arguments with each other all year long before that. It was like some feel-good classroom movie come true. (Klasovsky 2013)

Starting Peace Circles in Your Classroom

When you begin this work in your classroom, your students will need some introduction to prepare them to participate:

- Explain the circle purpose—to discuss issues, concerns, or accomplishments in a way that enables everyone to participate and to address the topic constructively.

- Explain the process—everyone sits in a circle, passing a talking piece from one person to the next. Taking a pass on speaking is OK if a person has nothing to add. Only the one holding the talking piece is allowed to speak. The talking piece should be an object that carries some symbolism for yourself or the class, to signal the importance of the discussion.

- Ask students to propose guidelines for the circle. These will generally include practices for any well-functioning small group in the classroom—listening, respecting differing viewpoints, "sharing the air," and maintaining confidentiality.

Some typical issues that circles can help classes to address:

- Exclusion of some students from particular small groups working on projects

- How students can be supportive of one another

- Bullying

- Hurtful gossip

- Understanding and accepting students who have disabilities (or better to say, differing abilities)

- Racial issues and other misunderstandings or misperceptions between social groups

- Gangs and neighborhood violence

- Particular incidents that trouble students or that require some action to help resolve them

- Celebration of class achievements and how they were accomplished

Connecting Peace Circles to Curriculum

You can connect the start of peace circles to English language arts curriculum by having students read an engaging novel on the subject. Ben Mikaelsen's *Touching Spirit Bear* is built around a community peace circle's effort to rehabilitate a violent fifteen-year-old boy by sending him to an isolated island off the southeast Alaskan coast for a year. Kids eleven years and up love this book.

Guiding a Circle

Start and end the circle with some kind of signal or activity that marks the boundaries of the process. The beginning can involve a brief one- or two-sentence check-in by each student. Then introduce the topic or issue that the circle is convened to address. If this is the first time the class is trying it and no specific issue has been troubling the atmosphere, you can begin with reflection on a recent class project or activity. One way a circle may end is with a round of brief reflections on how students felt about the discussion.

While discussion in a circle will depend on the issue or topic at hand, the teacher should use guiding questions to help move the discussion along and keep it constructive. Kay Pranis (2005) outlines purposes for questions the leader can ask:

- Encourage participants to speak from their own lived experience. For example: How have you been impacted? What has this situation been like for you? What has been the hardest thing for you? What do you need to move forward? What can you offer to help this situation?

- Invite participants to share stories from their lives—Share an experience when you . . .

- Focus on feelings and impacts rather than facts.

- Invite recognition of strengths or assets as well as difficulties.

- Transition participants (at an appropriate point) from the discussion of difficult or painful events into discussion of what can be done now to make things better.

If you're interested in further training for leading peace circles, check out these resources:

- Community Justice for Youth Institute, Chicago: http://cjyi.org/

- Peace Circles LLC, Fort Collins, CO : http://peacecircles.com/

- YWCA-MPLS, Minneapolis: www.ywcampls.org/our_voices/2012 /01/12/80/the_power_of_circle

- Center on Violence and Recovery, New York University: http:// centeronviolenceandrecovery.org/

- Partners in Restorative Initiatives, Rochester, NY: www.pirirochester.org/

- Teen Talking Circles, Seattle, WA: www.teentalkingcircles.org/index.php

- Peace Circle Center, Washington, DC: http://peacecirclecenter.org/

And if there's not an agency or training opportunity near you, handbooks, such as Kay Pranis' *The Little Book of Circle Processes* (2005), can provide self-training.

Once you are comfortable with leading circles, you can help other teachers get on board by modeling the conduct of a peace circle in other classrooms so teachers can see it in action with their own students, just as Mauricio Pineda did at Reilly School (see below).

Implementing Care Rooms

Care rooms are dedicated places where students can go to cool off when agitated or to seek counseling or support. Teachers and/or discipline staff can give special passes to students who are disruptive, instead of simply meting out punishment. Staffing can require some creativity. At Reilly School, the room has been staffed by a graduate education student. In some schools a care room can be part of the counseling office, since that's where struggling students often land anyway. A care room is essentially a counseling center in any case. Active counseling may sometimes be involved, but often a student just needs to be alone for a few minutes to calm down before returning to class. At Reilly, the room used for the peer council also serves as the care room location.

The school faculty will need to be thoroughly briefed on the role of the care room. The faculty and administration will need to set guidelines for teachers to be clear on when a problem involves a serious infraction that falls under a school's discipline policy and when it's appropriate to simply give the student a chance to gain his or her composure and get a bit of counseling support.

Implementing Conflict Resolution

Peer councils and peer mediation address problems once they have occurred, but they aren't designed to directly build school climate so that problems don't develop in the first place. Conflict resolution skills help students work out differences before they escalate into problematic behaviors. These are important skills for working together on social action projects, as well. The best conflict resolution programs address school climate broadly rather than only providing lessons on narrow behavioral skills.

Conflict Resolution Resources

Conflict resolution and peaceable school resources abound, and have been out there for many years. Here are descriptions of two to provide an idea of what they cover:

- Engaging Schools, Resolving Conflict Creatively Program (RCCP), http://engagingschools.org/?s=Resolving+Conflict+Creatively+Program. This program provides training for teachers to develop student skills in active listening, expressing feelings, dealing with anger, assertiveness, collaborative problem solving (including negotiation and mediation), appreciating diversity, and countering discrimination. Training is also provided for administrators, counselors, school staff, and parents, along with establishing a peer mediation team.

- Peace Education Foundation, www.peaceeducation.org/index.html. Training addresses community building, prosocial classroom behavior and de-escalation of conflicts, anger management, active listening, and communication skills.

These organizations charge fees for professional development, but they also publish materials that can be purchased for developing a program on your own.

An approach that integrates social skills more fully into the academic curriculum can be found in Nancy Steineke's *Reading and Writing Together* (2002) and in Nancy and Smokey Daniels' *Teaching the Social Skills of Academic Interaction* (2014). These books outline a multitude of classroom activities the authors have used over the years to help students work cooperatively in small groups and to encourage one another's learning rather than view school as competitive.

Unlike peace circles, peer council, and peer mediation, though, conflict resolution and community-building activities do not always involve students as the direct *initiators* for promoting change in their school community. This is not a bad thing. We teachers rightly have a passion for improving our schools, our classrooms, and the lives of our students. But the more we can coach and encourage the *students* to propose and establish new and better ways of repairing the world around them, the more we are truly empowering them for their present lives and their future.

RESTORATIVE JUSTICE GOES VIRAL

As with all of the work in this book, our hope is that students' engagement with social action will spill into every part of their lives, helping them not only to feel empowered but also to make positive changes in the world.

Restorative Justice Across the Curriculum and Around the School

Restorative justice practices can find a place in many subjects. As an art teacher, Mauricio Pineda guides his students to explore interpersonal issues in their art, so the walls of the school and the student art shows further promote the development of a supportive and just community school-wide. For a recent show, the sixth-grade students worked in small groups to identify problems they encounter in their lives, and each group chose one to represent artistically. The groups created "root cause" charts outlining the sources and implications of their problem (see Figure 6–7). They then sketched, using simple figures to represent people causing or being affected by the problem, and enacted tableaus while Pineda snapped pictures of them. The students used the pictures, in turn, to create sculptures to represent the causes and results of their problem (see Figure 6–8 for an example). Pineda even taught a unit on Giacometti to inspire the students to learn and use the sculptural style that he developed, so the students were learning a piece of art history in the process. Pineda is now leading peace circles in other classrooms and supporting fellow teachers as they begin to adopt them on their own.

Restorative Justice Reaching Beyond the School

Once teachers and students see the value of restorative justice, they often begin to consider taking it out to the wider community—thus bringing them to full-on social action. For example, Mauricio Pineda is contemplating placing student art in businesses around the neighborhood, with students giving short talks about their art pieces as customers stop in. Additionally, the Reilly School peer council students have envisioned their own next step. As council member Carolina Flores remarked, "I'm really proud of what we've achieved, but we want to go above and beyond, and not just in the school." Her fellow members chimed in, proposing workshops for parents, asking the principal to explain restorative justice in meetings with parents, and spearheading new peer councils when they go off to high school. One's hope for the future of our communities leaps when hearing young people talk like this.

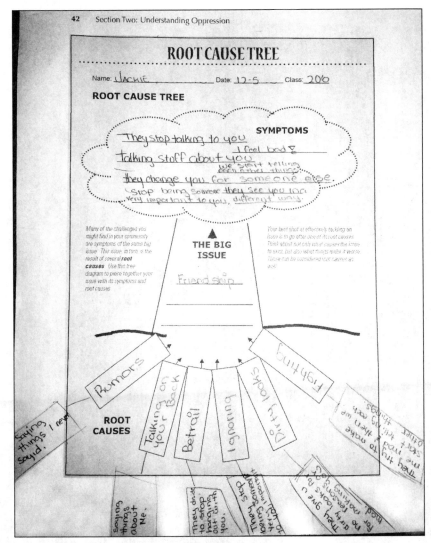

ROOT CAUSE TREE

Name: JACKIE   Date: 12-5   Class: 206

ROOT CAUSE TREE

SYMPTOMS

They stop talking to you
                    I feel bad &
talking stuff about you
                    we stent telling
                    each other things
they change you for someone else.
stop being someone they see you in a
very important to you. different way.

Many of the challenges you might find in your community are symptoms of the same big issue. This issue, in turn, is the result of several *root causes*. Use this tree diagram to piece together your issue with its symptoms and root causes.

▲ THE BIG ISSUE

Friendship

Your best shot at effectively tackling an issue is to go after one of its root causes. Think about not only what causes the issue to exist, but also what things make it worse. These can be considered root causes as well.

Rumors
Talking on your Back
Betrail
Ignoring
Dirty looks
Fighting

ROOT CAUSES

saying things I never sayid.

saying things about Me.

They didn't want to stop hanging around you.

the reason they act dirty looks u

Tho give u no reason bad for no reasons.

They try hard to make them start telling other things

Figure 6–7 Root Cause Tree, Reilly School Art Project

Figure 6–8 Giacometti-Style Sculpture, Reilly School Art Project

SOCIAL ACTION IN THE SCHOOL THROUGH RESTORATIVE JUSTICE ▪ 139

7
~

GROWING AN AFTER-SCHOOL PROGRAM

No surprise, after-school social action programs look very much like the classrooms described in previous chapters. But while teaching with inquiry and community action is great for the classroom, there are some real advantages to conducting projects after school:

- You won't have to worry that you aren't covering required curriculum.
- You and the students won't be restricted by test prep or other demands (well, at least not as often as the classes are).
- You can involve students from multiple classrooms and grade levels. Older students become mentors for younger group members.
- It can be easier to bring on board other teachers whose class schedules differ from yours.
- Such highly meaningful extracurricular activity not only looks good on a student's college application, but focuses kids' after-school time on truly worthwhile effort.

Yes, you already have a lot on your plate. But this kind of work can inspire students and help you to realize some of the big-picture goals that brought you into teaching in the first place. In some schools, doing action civics after school may in fact be the only way to get a project going. You and your students *can* strive to change the world. You *can* help kids to grow and learn while doing real, meaningful work. You *can* help students to see themselves as agents of change in the world.

Of course, there are considerations particular to after-school groups, and the experience of Chicago's Alcott College Prep High School Social Justice League, guided by English teacher Heather Van Benthuysen, highlights some of those.

WHAT AN AFTER-SCHOOL CLUB CAN ACHIEVE

At Alcott the Social Justice League students at all four grade levels meet weekly after school to investigate issues within the school, planning and executing actions to help improve it as a learning institution. The group has played an active role in the life of the school, even providing input on selection of a new principal.

Identifying School-Wide Concerns

Just about any social or community issue can be fair game for an after-school club, but it's not surprising that many such groups zero in on needs that cut across their whole school. Heather emphasizes that it's important to guide students to take on something actionable. The Alcott Social Justice League was especially motivated to address the culture and climate of their school after an evaluation conducted by the school board revealed that Alcott students were particularly unhappy with relationships among various social groups in the school. The Social Justice League team spent a series of meetings poring over the survey data—so choosing an issue and starting their research took place simultaneously.

But while the kids agreed on the general issue, their initial brainstorm about possible solutions revealed a wide range of opinions as to what it was actually about. Heather therefore invited them to construct a "root cause tree" on the chalkboard. This graphic asks students to articulate the causes of a problem as well as the resulting effects (see Figure 6–7 and Mikva Challenge 2015, pp. 104–108). Heather finds it an invaluable tool, and even when it identifies multiple contributing forces, students usually recognize one that they consider most important to address. In this case, the exercise enabled the students to think more deeply about the social disconnects in the school, and revealed that they were actually in agreement on many aspects of the problem. Then, when the league held a forum on the Ferguson, Missouri, situation and no other Alcott students attended, they grew firmly resolved to do something to improve student involvement in issues that mattered.

Conducting Research in Public

To help everyone focus on school climate, Alcott's Social Justice League held four events over the course of the 2013–2014 academic year for panels of experts to share their knowledge in open forums at which the student audience could direct questions. Their research, in other words, was shared with interested fellow students as it took place. The first three forums dealt with engaging instruction, but the fourth focused more directly on school culture and climate. The league invited a number of education experts to that final event: a University of Chicago professor with expertise in school research, curriculum developers from social action organizations, a teacher who developed another school's restorative justice program, and their own school's dean of discipline.

Figure 7–1 shows the letter that league students drafted and sent to faculty and administrators.

Figure 7–1 League Letter

Hello Alcott Faculty and Staff,

We would like to formally invite you to our Panel on School Culture & Climate. This year we are researching effective ways we can improve our culture and climate at Alcott College Prep. We've been making significant strides toward our end-goal of producing the best climate and culture we can for our beloved school.

A main component of this effort is research. We've scoured the Internet, taken reliable notes, and have used previous data to narrow our actions and develop focus areas specialized for Alcott and schools alike. We would be grateful if you came and shared your knowledge in this important and all too often ignored aspect of our community. The learning, ideas, and insight you share with us and our fellow Wildcats will contribute to our proposal to administration and inspire others to help us make a change.

This will take place on May 13 in room 106 at 4:30. We welcome your presence to help us explore solutions to this issue. If you have any questions or concerns, please feel free to contact us at alcottsjl@gmail.com.

Sincerely and gratefully,
Alcott College Prep's *Social Justice League*

The group conducted an online survey of fellow students as well, and each team member took the answers to one of the questions to analyze and report back to the group.

Launching a Multiyear, School-Wide Effort

With students from all grade levels, an after-school group can more easily organize whole-school activities. Projects conducted by an after-school club can readily continue beyond the end of a single school year, and the expanded time allows for larger efforts. The Alcott League decided the next fall to tackle a number of elements in the school culture: student relationships with their teachers and with each other, a sense of who they are as a student body, and an understanding of the school's mission and what makes the school special. So they launched a series of events to address these things:

- Conducting a student panel on student voice at an open house for new students and their families at the start of the year.

- Converting the traditional Chicago hazing tradition of "Freshie Friday," at which older students threw pennies at freshmen, into a "High Five Freshie Friday."

- Posting student "thought bubbles" on a wall in the school.

- Drafting and publishing a set of "Civic Goals and Agreements" to articulate the values and practices promoted by the League (see Figure 7–2).

- Holding a "culture and climate" week with discussion questions and ice-breaker activities for the homerooms, encouragement for students to join school clubs, and wall posters featuring the "Civic Goals and Agreements" that had been drafted, along with student statements about what Alcott should be like four years from now.

- Leading an assembly on the vision and mission of the school, at which all the teachers introduced themselves, and students volunteered to testify about how the school had changed and improved.

- Helping organize an assembly celebrating the school's recognition as a "Democracy School" by the McCormick Foundation (see Chapter 8 for more on this).

- Promoting the "Soap Box" speech competition sponsored by the Mikva Challenge, in which students compete within their school and then city-wide in Chicago. It has grown at Alcott to include all freshman and sophomore English classes and some upper-level courses as well.

Figure 7-2 Alcott College Prep Civic Goals and Agreements

As a Democracy School we will:

1. Show tolerance and respect.

2. Appreciate our differences.

3. Reject violence.

4. Commit to finding a balance between our personal liberties and our social responsibility to others.

5. Make sure everyone feels like they belong to our community; value the voice of all members of our community equally.

6. Show that we value community and community involvement.

7. Engage in respectful dialogue with those who hold different points of view (speak and listen and learn equally).

8. Actively learn about, discuss, and act on social issues and civic matters, issues, the news, etc.

9. Believe that a democracy is as good as what its people put into it—so we will continue to work and grow and improve our school by committing to the above stated dispositions.

- Organizing a series of "Open Minds Open Mic" after-school events at which students get to speak on one of several issues identified through an online survey (Scenes from the first of these are shown in Figure 7-3).

- Giving recognition awards to students nominated by their peers for contributions to student voice, civil discourse, civic action, and a culture of respect for one another.

- Serving directly on the school's Climate and Culture Committee alongside faculty representatives from each department.

All this helped to stir wider faculty involvement as well—more about that in Chapter 8.

Not every after-school group will be ready to take on such an ambitious agenda. This club had been growing and building confidence and expertise for three years. Taking on one or two initiatives could be plenty for a new group to consider, research, plan, and execute.

Figure 7–3 Alcott "Open Minds Open Mic" Event to Promote Civil Discourse

The Teacher's Role in an After-School Social Action Club

Although Heather pioneered the after-school work at Alcott, the group grew more independent as it gained experience and insight. Once that the group was established, Heather intervened most often just to remind these eager young people to investigate thoroughly before jumping to conclusions about the reasons a problem exists, an action to take, or their readiness to execute it. As students work through their plans for an action or event they may have a great many details to figure out. They'll need to talk through these and make their own decisions, which can take several meetings just to hash out. And sometimes they need help reaching a conclusion.

The Alcott students, for instance, struggled with the agenda of their first "Open Minds Open Mic" event at which members of the student body could voice their ideas on issues that mattered to them. Should it focus on a single topic, offer a choice of three or four, or simply leave the agenda open to whatever issues students wanted to bring up? Group members mulled a number of rationales—being welcoming and open to the interests of the students who attend, versus giving the discussion a coherent shape. While team members shared a variety of thoughtful observations, they were making little progress toward a resolution—not so much because they disagreed, but because they lacked criteria for weighing one idea against another. Seeing this, Heather urged them to recall their original purpose for holding the event—to promote student involvement and civil discourse on issues facing the school. She also helped them think about how students might respond to the invitation. Would an open agenda encourage participation or leave things unfocused? Would specified topics constrict people's participation or spark their thoughts? The team was then able to settle on conducting an online survey to identify preferred issues, which would then provide the agenda for the event. Open discussion plus a gentle teacher intervention at the right moment helped to make the team's deliberations productive.

On deeper, more socially significant issues, a teacher's careful questioning may be important, however. If the league students had started blaming fellow students for their passivity, rather than seeking avenues for engaging them, it would have been important to urge them to investigate why this was happening.

Increased Student Confidence

Anyone visiting an Alcott Social Justice League meeting will see just how reflective and confident the students have grown as they've worked together over two to three years. Here's what several team members had to say about it:

> **Bea:** *I like working with other students, building relationships with them. I like the diversity, and getting to know kids from other grade levels. . . . I want more students to have this life-changing experience. It gives you confidence and makes you stand up for your own opinions.*

Kristine: *It's good to know that I'm part of something and making a change in the community. . . . We wanted to improve the culture of the school, but we didn't know how. People had different ideas about how to do it. But when we filled in the root cause tree we realized that a lot of our ideas were the same. . . . What's important is that learning is a two-way street. It's impossible to learn without having your own voice. But you also have to listen, too.*

DJ: *When I came to this school as a freshman no one knew me, and there was no one to help me. Lots of kids complained and didn't like it here. I don't want new freshmen feeling the way we felt. Now I feel constantly energized about how we're growing as a team. I'm more confident about my leadership and collaborating abilities. I feel like my ideas matter. I hope I can bring the lessons I've learned here wherever I go to college.*

MAKING AN AFTER-SCHOOL CLUB WORK

Many of the steps in an after-school club's efforts will be much the same as those described in Chapters 1 through 4 in this book. However, there are also a number of tasks to consider for an after-school setting. With the Alcott team in mind as an example of how a group can succeed, here are some steps that are particular to after-school social action clubs.

Build Support Within the School

Of course, you can start an after-school program on your own. But having partners and a supportive understanding with the school administration can make a tremendous difference. Just as with restorative justice, building support is an important first step, and time spent on it will pay off down the line. So be sure to use the one-on-one discussions outlined in the previous chapter to gain understanding and allies.

One way to build your club is to work with an already existing activity in your school. Service learning programs offer a good possibility when they are robust and not just about students collecting hours for a requirement. But they need to involve real study, action, and reflection—that is, they need to include "learning" and "action" as well as "service." And your contribution can be to help the students consider more impactful ways to make a difference, valuing and promoting systemic changes—even if they're small—in a community. Community service is valuable and important, but your goal is for your students to address community *change*.

Having launched student action groups at several schools, Heather Van Benthuysen finds that each situation presents its own challenges and opportunities. At one school, the principal was not supportive and other teachers were lukewarm. But Heather simply began recruiting the more outspoken students, who were happy to join because they felt no one seemed to care about what they had to say. Once one or two were involved, they began to bring friends along. As a small group of five, the students decided to tackle the racial divide in the student body by holding a "diversity week" focused on appreciative inquiry. They shared thoughts on their identities and values. They created a "communi-tree" on which fellow students attached leaves, each holding a statement about one thing they promised to do for the school. The group searched the web for lesson plans on diversity for each subject and offered these to the teachers. When they went before the faculty to thank them for their support (even though it wasn't universal), they grew emotional, impressing the adults with their seriousness and providing a turning point that gave the effort momentum.

At another school, students were doubtful that their start-up could succeed. But the principal and dean asked for help with low attendance, so the team conducted a survey to learn about causes and possible solutions. The survey responses surprised everyone: while adults assumed the kids didn't care about their education, the biggest problems were the lack of safety walking to school and dirty uniforms that students were ashamed to put on. Newly energized and appreciated, the team planned weekly after-school "laundry days" at which kids could get their uniforms washed.

Seek an External Partner

Brian Brady and Jill Bass, the Executive Director and Director of Curriculum and Teacher Development, respectively, at Mikva Challenge (the Chicago-based organization that encourages youth to become community leaders), advise that community partners are a great help in achieving success in action projects, and after-school groups are especially likely to be in need of support. Naturally, one-on-one meetings are the tool of choice for recruiting these partners. Organization leaders can help you obtain resources, open doors for meeting local officials, and help you and the students understand how decision making works in your community. And they will come to greatly appreciate your students, your teaching, and your school in the process—no small victory in itself. What kinds of partners might these be? In Chicago, the Juvenile Justice Council, a student-based, citywide after-school group sponsored by Mikva, has drawn on a range of community resources:

- Heartland Alliance is a Chicago-based antipoverty group that works on housing, health care, economic opportunity, and legal issues.

- Outreach Youth Services provides a variety of support services for teens, including help with the justice system, in a number of Chicago neighborhoods and suburbs.

- Illinois Collaboration on Youth builds capacity for other youth service or-ganizations and collaborates with these organizations to advocate for poli-cies that more effectively serve teens.

- Adler School of Professional Psychology provided experts who briefed the council on psychological issues for teenagers who need help to lead more productive lives.

- The Cook County governing board, whose president asked Mikva to create the Juvenile Justice Council.

At Chicago's Marie Curie High School, when history teacher Adam Heenan's stu-dents decided to explore and take action on the issue of homelessness, they partnered with the Chicago Coalition for the Homeless. That organization even grants scholarships for graduating high school seniors who are or have been homeless. Plots in the Ecology Club's garden at Prosser High School are supported by a number of local churches, and a law office has contributed labor and refreshments on garden "build days." Every com-munity has its own nonprofit groups focused on social issues and needs. These groups are almost always eager to inform and support students.

Raise Funds

You can do this work on the cheap if necessary, but resources can make a big differ-ence. While the Internet has become more and more powerful for student investigation of community issues, actual hard-copy books, newspapers, and print materials remain useful in the digital age, and obtaining them requires some funds. Student-created pam-phlets and posters may be needed in a campaign for policy change. Transportation may be necessary for attending government agency meetings. Snacks to keep kids going after school are not just a frill; they signal your concern for Maslow's hierarchy of needs. And it wouldn't hurt for you to actually be paid for your professional after-school time. So if your school doesn't have money for this (even though it should), where can you go to seek monetary support?

- Many schools and districts have local education support organizations. For example, in Evanston, Illinois, Foundation 65 raises funds and provides grants for a variety of teachers' special projects in the elementary district.

- Neighborhood organizations that share an interest in your students' cho-sen issue may be happy to help, either with funds or with what funders call "in-kind" support—that is, actual materials or services rather than money. High-profile topics like juvenile justice and preventing recidivism are espe-cially likely to gain the attention of community organizations.

- Kickstarter and other similar websites enable people to seek funds from interested people anywhere, for a wide variety of appealing projects. Recently on this site we found proposals for art and mural workshops, the composing of choral music for special education students, and a smartphone app that promotes reading—and all had contributions mounting up. With Kickstarter, you set a goal for the amount to be raised and a deadline date. If you reach or exceed your goal you receive the funds. If you don't, the pledges from your supporters get canceled. Other crowdfunding sites like Indiegogo don't require this reach-it-or-lose-it strategy.

- The Donors Choose website is similar to Kickstarter, though it usually leads to a connection between a teacher seeking supplies or other small levels of help and one or several donors who take an interest in the project. Just a few of the hundreds of requests on the site as of this writing include habitats for small animals for an environment project, a digital camera to record events at the school, a soil test kit for a science project, and recycling bins and a bulletin board to promote recycling in the school.

At Prosser High School, Marnie Ware is continually applying for small grants that have enabled the group to build a shelter and raised garden beds, purchase seedlings, and hold community "build days" to expand their garden. For Heather Van Benthuysen, the district-wide emphasis on improving school culture led the district to provide a grant for student voice activities, and the team used the funds to purchase an improved sound system, publicity materials, and T-shirts for their "Open Minds Open Mic" events.

Funders for education projects can be found in communities around the country, so don't hesitate to research the opportunities wherever you teach. Here are just a few examples:

- Plus Endowment, Paris, TN (www.facebook.com/plusendowment)

- Central Columbia Foundation, Bloomsburg, PA (www.centralcolumbia
  .k12.pa.us/domain/42)

- Fairfield Foundation for Education, Fairfield, CT (www.fairfieldffe.org
  /home.cfm)

- Captain Planet Foundation, Atlanta, GA, focused on environmental issues
  (http://captainplanetfoundation.org/apply-for-grants/)

- RGK Foundation, Austin, TX (www.rgkfoundation.org/public/guidelines)

Recruit Students

Now you need the kids. When you're working with a class the students are simply there, in your room, but after-school groups must be gathered from all over the building. When Heather was starting the Alcott College Prep Social Justice League, she visited homerooms across the school and spoke with individual students she knew to be potential leaders. She held informational after-school meetings where snacks were served. And since she was already conducting projects in her own classes that included social and community action, it was natural to invite students who were especially enthusiastic about them. It took just a few months to gather her initial group. As with her experience at previous schools, the planning and execution of an initial event created the buzz needed to get things rolling. In this case, the team's first action was to convince the local school council (a local community governing board that exists at each Chicago public school) that students should interview candidates for the open principalship position. As community organizers tell us, a quick win like this can be great for establishing credibility and momentum.

Team Building

Of course, building a supportive culture is essential in any classroom, but it's especially needed in after-school groups because students coming from multiple grade levels may arrive with very little connection to one another. In a classroom, most students will go along and participate in a project since it's expected as part of the work, but an after-school group is dependent on the continuing excitement and sense of belonging that you must help to generate. The ongoing work of a club calls for collaboration, occasional disagreement, and struggle, so the group needs to have a basis of trust and commitment that enables the members to manage their inevitable challenges. There's an endless supply of get-acquainted ice-breaker activities on the Internet. You'll find several extensive lists at www.cre8iowa.org/2014/10/01/team-building-activities/. For ongoing reinvigoration, Heather Van Benthuysen suggests the following favorites.

Appreciative Inquiry

Most of Heather's techniques are rooted in appreciative inquiry, the process of learning about and building on the best in people and the organizations and conditions around them. For an appreciative inquiry exercise on leadership, for example, she asks students to think of a person they know who has shown leadership and to share stories about him or her. The group then brainstorms a list of the leadership qualities illustrated in the stories. Finally they address the question, "What do we need to do to promote these qualities in ourselves?"

Recognizing a Variety of Skills

Another of Heather's favorites is what she calls an "asset bank." Once a group decides on an action to influence some change or improvement in the community, each group member offers a skill or commitment to help in some way. Students can also suggest a particular group member who they believe possesses a needed talent. "All students," Heather asserts, "need the opportunity to be the best person they can be."

Students' Own Gentle Reminders

Heather uses a "magic word" trick to enable students to encourage each other when the going gets rough. At the start of the year, she invites students to choose a word that they can use as a reminder to anyone who puts down a fellow student, or otherwise acts in a way detrimental to the positive culture of the class or club. It can be used as well to celebrate a positive development. Over their initial weeks together, students brainstorm possibilities, discuss and debate them, and finally vote on their word for the year. The word enables students to gently steer one another in a positive direction without putting anyone on the defensive.

High Fives

Heather makes sure that at the start and end of an activity, whether or not it's finished or successful, students high-five about it. She and the students talk about this, and she agrees that it's rather dorky, but stresses that the symbolism of regular support and celebration is necessary. As she puts it, "I do tons of team building and leadership coaching. It is a constant need, and I learn more every year—heck, every week." And frequently, these being teenagers, it's important to simply stop and have fun for a few minutes.

Reflection

Strong groups use reflection to both value their effort and consider ways to get better at working together and supporting one another. Good questions to ask:

- How did we work together as a team?
- Who took the lead in solving a problem?
- How did team members communicate with one another?
- How did the team formulate a plan to solve the problem?

When teachers hand over decision making to students, those students may not always make the best choices in planning or execution. However, if they take time to reflect afterward, analyzing what they did well and what needed improvement, they will learn and grow stronger, and develop the habits that will enable their continued growth as well.

RESOURCES FOR INFORMATION, STRATEGIES, AND TRAINING

All teachers can benefit from professional development and expertise to help them implement learning with social action. But those embarking on after-school clubs especially need support, since they do this work in addition to their regular classroom commitments, must carry out extra tasks to make a program successful, and may need help convincing school administrators to support it. Fortunately, as more and more communities recognize the need for active civic commitment, the number of resources and teachers' learning opportunities continue to grow. Here are the most well known of these groups.

- Center for Civic Education and its program, Project Citizen, offers workshops in a variety of locations across the country, with coordinators in forty-four states. The center also publishes full textbooks on civic education for middle and high school.

- CIRCLE (www.civicyouth.org) conducts research on many aspects of civics education and youth involvement in civic efforts. Most of its reports are downloadable. Check out its working paper—"Building an Evidence-Based Practice of Action Civics"—which makes the case for social action projects in a concise and convincing way (www.civicyouth.org/wp-content /uploads/2013/08/WP_78_Gingold.pdf).

- Constitutional Rights Foundation (http://crf-usa.org) conducts workshops for teachers and lessons specifically designed for civics courses but applicable in other subjects as well. It's based in California, with special programs for California teachers. A separate but related group, the Constitutional Rights Foundation Chicago, operates in that city.

- Earth Force (www.earthforce.org) promotes student groups and schools addressing environmental concerns in fifty-two communities in the United States and Canada. It provides program activity outlines and brief examples of successful projects in a number of schools, plus a few detailed inquiry activities. Contact the group to obtain detailed curriculum guides.

- Generation Citizen (http://generationcitizen.org), with offices in Boston, New York, Providence, and the San Francisco Bay Area, supports social action learning. The program provides trained volunteer college students as coaches. Even if you're not in their area, their statement of principles can be helpful in conceptualizing community action programs.

- The Institute for Community Research (www.incommunityresearch. org) supports a variety of programs on action-based research by youth. It has published several books that offer strategies and curricula for action-oriented research on community problems.

- Mikva Challenge (www.mikvachallenge.org) is a model in Chicago for citywide development of civic action for youth. Summer workshops draw teachers from across the country. Mikva sponsors citywide as well as school-based councils, involves students in voter registration, and places student interns in elected officials' offices. Its curriculum guide, *Issues to Action*, can take you through the full process of conducting an inquiry and social action project in your classroom or after school. Mikva's website alone is an outstanding resource.

- National Action Civics Collaborative (http://actioncivicscollaborative.org) brings together the organizations listed here to promote their work, hold conferences, and so on.

- National Youth Leadership Council (www.nylc.org) is the largest organization focused on service learning. The best of service learning programs involve learning based on teaching with social action. The organization's standards stress student voice and leadership, in-depth research on issues, and robust action in the community, as opposed to one-day service-oriented field trips. Its website provides a range of articles and webinars on issues and strategies for effective service learning.

- The University Community Collaborative (http://uccollab.org), working in Philadelphia through Temple University, supports youth leadership and voice at a number of levels.

- Youth On Board (www.youthonboard.org), based in Boston, sponsors the Boston Student Advisory Council, which is composed of high school students from across the city and provides youth voice on education and community issues. Youth On Board also offers training and consultation in schools around the country, for both educators and student leaders. The organization publishes curriculum materials and guides for working with youth and connecting them with community decision makers.

Here's one more story to remind us how naturally learning with social action can germinate and blossom in an after-school club, even without a teacher leading the way.

Sixth-grade language arts teacher Laurie Hendrickson and sixth-grade math teacher Mary Spyropoulos are the faculty advisors for the robotics club at Roosevelt Middle School in River Forest, a suburb west of Chicago. Along with creating robotic machines to compete against other schools, robotics teams competing in the First Lego League are required to complete a research report and demonstrate their team's ability to cooperate. Last year's theme was "Nature's Fury" and the Roosevelt team decided to focus on flooding of the Des Plaines River, which bisects the town, because the homes of many team members were subject to the floods. Since teams are required to develop a solution to a problem, prove it can work, and present it to some outside audience, the students invited the town director of public works and the chair of the local Citizens' Corps Council to meet with them. As the students explained in their summary report for the area competition:

> 7 of 10 team members have had their homes flooded in the past three years. Since we love superheroes, we hoped to find one perfect superhero solution to River Forest's flooding problem. When we first presented our "Super Solution: Using Water to Fight Water," to the Director of Public Works for the Village of River Forest, he immediately shot it down. We all gasped when he told us why; bad guys could vandalize our water-filled tubes, causing more damage. It was straight out of a comic book! Although we felt like all of our early research had gone to waste, we kept working and found out that in our village everyone needs to work together to prevent flooding and property damage. Thus, our motto became: "Be Your Own Superhero."

The students went on to create a checklist of ways to prepare for and limit damage from local flooding. This was pulled together from information scattered across various parts of the village website. They also prepared a flowchart for diagnosing problems and vulnerabilities in flood-prone homes, which—as the students explained—could save homeowners the cost of obtaining an engineer to do the job. The officials returned to the school to hear the students' final presentation. And the improved checklist can now be found on the village website at www.vrf.us/residents/flooding.

Teachers did not plan this project. It's the *kids* who chose the issue and initiated the effort. The *kids* contacted the village authorities and invited them to speak with the team. The *kids* researched, sought help, and revised their plan. And it's the *kids* who conducted the work to improve the well-being of their community. Community action grew from their concern while the teachers' role was to stand by and celebrate their effort. Translating learning into social action doesn't get any better than that.

PROMOTING CHANGE
IN SCHOOLS

As a teacher who cares about empowering students as active
and responsible community members, you probably want to see more
of this going on beyond your own classroom. It's less fun doing this
kind of teaching alone. And if teachers in earlier grades are guiding
projects with social action, you won't be starting from scratch when the
kids reach you. They'll already have many of the skills they need to do a
great job (though being young people with still-developing brains, they
may need some reminding and deepening of their thinking).

Change in organizations like schools, however, is usually a complex
process. Many people, teachers included, are easily threatened by something new, especially if they think it implies that somehow they weren't
already doing their best. And if it involves letting go of some control, as
good social action projects do, it can seem downright dangerous:

- What if the kids don't do the work and just fool around?

- That's great, but I don't believe *my* kids can do this.

- What if I don't get to "cover" all the standards and I end up with a low evaluation?

- How will I be able to keep track of everything the students are doing and learning—or not learning?

- Is this too political? Maybe I'd get in trouble for it.

- This is not what I was trained to do. It just sounds hard!

Then there are all the mandates, standards, looming state tests, overstuffed curriculum guides, doubting and overstressed colleagues, and scheduling limitations that present obstacles to more in-depth, student- and community-responsive learning experiences. Of course, there are ways to cope with these challenges, and they are part of the strategizing needed to get social action projects going more widely.

Now, perhaps you teach in a school with a wonderfully supportive principal who helps deal with these obstacles and leads teachers to develop new approaches collaboratively—that's great! But maybe you work in a place where valuable new ideas have come and gone without ever taking root, and colleagues have grown understandably cynical, or suspicious of your motives. So if you are going to successfully promote change and not get rejected or just plain burned out, you'll need to be strategic.

Fortunately, there's help available. The people called community organizers, though maligned by some who really have no idea what they do, have been learning and working for decades to help organizations and communities change, with much success. Trouble is, most teachers have never needed to learn about these strategies. One education activist recalls his own moment of dawning realization that he needed to think more strategically about his efforts. A community organizer he was working with asked one day, "So your writing project provides workshops for teachers. But what does your overall campaign look like?"

Hmmm. Campaign. He said that he'd never used that word. To the organizer, a campaign had a beginning, middle, and an end, allies and opponents, opportunities and obstacles, and a variety of possible strategies for change, with "workshops" being just one out of a grab-bag. He never thought the same way about working in a school after that.

MAKING CHANGE WORK IN YOUR SCHOOL

So what are some strategies an organizer might suggest for getting more teachers to conduct projects with social action? Let's take a look.

Sit Down One-on-One with Fellow Teachers

A story heard from a teacher not long ago:

I often send my students to the school library for inquiry projects, but for a long time the librarian would never help out. She always had an excuse. Then I decided to start dropping by the library in the mornings before school. I'd just chat with the librarian for a few minutes, and ask about her work and books she liked. Suddenly one day she offered, "You know those projects you have your kids do? Maybe I could give you a hand with the library research." I was stunned.

To expand on the description outlined in Chapter 6, a one-on-one meeting is a discussion with one other person to learn about his or her thinking and values, and to share your own. Organizers view one-on-one conversations as the most important tool at their disposal. They provide opportunities to build positive professional relationships. Any request for help to advance your learning-with-social-action effort should wait for a later occasion, after you know enough to connect it with the other person's particular interests and strengths. This can take time, especially if you need to hold a series of such sessions with faculty members—but it's time well spent because you'll gradually learn who supports your effort and what questions need to be answered for the doubters.

One-on-one meetings with friendly colleagues are almost always surprising because you'll learn things about them that you never knew and discover experiences and values you didn't realize you share. Fortunately, the same thing almost always happens with people who *don't* agree with you. We come to our work really caring about children and about making a difference for them. This can easily get buried in the politics and crush of life in a school. But a conversation about the paths that took each of you into teaching and your hopes for the kids can bring both of you back to essentials, even when you differ on some issues. You need to make sure, though, that your listening communicates a level of respect in addition to the support for one another that may develop.

One-on-one meetings are more than just friendly chats. They will probably involve sharing personal histories, but they are essentially professional. They enable you to learn about what matters to the other person professionally, and where you might find common ground. And they provide some safety—there's no larger audience to hear if the two of you disagree. If you do find yourself on the topic of teaching and learning with social action, you may at least learn what doubts or concerns the person has, and be better able to respond to them in the future.

If Your Prospective Partner Is Leery

One frequently asked question: "What if I propose coffee with a colleague and she's not interested, or actively suspicious about the whole idea?" You might say: "Look, we debate about things in meetings, but I would like to understand a little bit better where you're coming from. We work together in this building so it might help if we knew more about each other, professionally." Then, during your conversation, remember your real goal: learning about the person and his or her beliefs, and sharing yours—not trying to sell a project. Suspend your judgment. Just get curious.

Next Steps

So you've had your one-on-one with your critics and friends and it went pretty well, you think. But then, what comes next? This depends on what you learn. You may conclude that you can partner with a couple of other teachers or a grade-level team to pilot a project and report on your successes. You may decide there's enough support to bring a proposal to an instructional leadership team. You might realize you need to provide answers to some of your critics' concerns. Or you may decide to gather more data on your students' learning through a project before going any further. Whatever you decide, your strategy will be well informed.

Build Support with the Principal

It's a no-brainer how crucial the principal can be for the success of your change effort, so this step has appeared repeatedly in this book. One-on-one meetings with the principal are of course a good way to start. They'll probably be short, considering the job pressures on school administrators these days. But any request you have for support is much more likely to be heard sympathetically if you've built a base of trust and mutual knowledge first. And if you know where you share common ground, you can (later on) build your case on that.

Considering your principal's interests and goals wouldn't hurt either. What was this person's previous experience before taking on the job at your school? Most principals began as teachers, so what subject(s) or grade levels did this principal teach? What are his or her passions and interests in or outside of school? What issues are uppermost in guiding the school, for this leader? What kind of help or support might he or she especially appreciate from you?

Once you are ready to ask the principal to support a wider social action effort, it's a good idea to base your request on concerns or priorities that he or she has.

- If your principal relies on data to make decisions, you'll need some on student learning as a result of your social action projects (See the Core Thinking and Research on Teaching and Learning with Social Action section in the resources at the end of this book for some help with this.).

- If he or she emphasizes critical reading skills, bring along lesson plans to show how your projects incorporate these.

After this initial meeting, keep an open line of communication with your principal about the progress you're making, and advocate for your students and their work together when necessary so you can ensure that the students continue to own the work. A cautionary tale from a friend illustrates how sensitive the process can be.

> *I once worked with a school's instructional leadership team which decided, after consultation with the rest of the faculty, to focus on students' thinking skills. This seemed like a great idea and elicited a lot of faculty support. The team identified a professional book they thought would be helpful; but the principal surprised us by reading it over the summer (though she'd never shown much interest in curriculum in the past), and grew so enthusiastic that she declared everyone in the building must follow its principles. From then on, the instructional leadership team faded away. Members stopped coming to meetings. After all, if the principal was going to make all the decisions, what was the point in being involved? We had to regroup.*

Get Help and Support from Outside Sources

Organizations and experts on education with social action can be of great help and add to the credibility of your effort—as long as they are introduced in a way that respects the work of the teachers in your building. Chapter 7 provides a list of organizations that offer information, curriculum materials, workshops, and other kinds of support for teaching and learning with social action. But other sources also exist. Faculty members at a number of universities and schools around the country teach relevant courses, conduct research, and can lend expertise to help promote this kind of education. You might turn to institutions in your region, or look online for support. You can find many active educators and researchers on the Facebook page "Student Voice Research and Practice"—www.facebook.com/groups/studentvoicepage/—which lists over 650 members.

Arrange Cross-Classroom or Cross-School Visits

It helps tremendously for teachers to see a project in action, so they can visualize it in their own classrooms and observe at least some of the teaching moves that make it go well. At the same time, it's wise to plan carefully, taking into account the social dynamics among the faculty. Here are some strategic matters to consider.

- If visits are to a classroom in your school, you'll need to ensure that the teacher serving as a model doesn't get labeled as the golden girl/guy or administrator's pet. One way to avoid this is to arrange for visits to a number of classrooms, with host teachers soliciting advice from their visitors afterward, rather than just serving as superstars.

- If visiting another school, select one with students similar to those in your building. Otherwise it will be easy for your colleagues to claim that "these kids" are just better behaved or more academically advanced than their own. Sharing data on the students' preproject attitudes or achievement can show that the schools are actually comparable. They may seem different only because the students immersed in projects become so highly engaged in their work.

- Make visits more productive by scheduling debriefing time with the host teachers during a planning period or after school. The hosts can explain how they organize the projects and how the work has improved student learning. And the visitors can ask plenty of questions so they come away with confidence that they can do this too. It's good to ask the host teachers to prepare so the visitors get as much useful information as possible. Follow-up discussions back at your school can keep the process moving.

Jill Bass, curriculum developer at Mikva Challenge, explains that in visits she guides, teachers get to see the many small strategies that expert teachers use to help things go smoothly. After one visit, for example, a relatively new teacher who worked with a challenging student population was inspired to rearrange the seating in her room so it better facilitated engagement among her students. Jill finds that observed teachers benefit as well. The very presence of observers makes a teacher more conscious of her practice and recommitted to working at the top of her game. Debriefing sessions provide an opportunity for the observed teacher to talk about her work, an activity for which there's little time in the normal school day.

Jill uses several guides and response forms to help make a classroom visit as productive as possible:

- An introduction to the purposes and procedures of the visit (see Figure 8–1)

- A previsit form for the host teacher to outline his or her objectives for the lesson, the activities that will take place, and particular elements for the visitor to watch for

- A previsit form for the visitor(s) to consider what he or she hopes to get from the experience

- A debriefing guide and forms for the host and visiting teachers to jot reflections during discussion

Figure 8–1 Mikva Challenge Classroom Visit Guidelines

MIKVA CHALLENGE CLASSROOM VISIT OVERVIEW

Classroom Visits: The Purpose

First, these are visits—not evaluations. **The purpose of these visits is for professional growth.** This growth happens for visitor and teacher being visited.

- For the visiting teacher—the context of another teacher's classroom is a rich environment to reflect on your own practice. You will set guiding questions for yourself to help focus your visit.

- For the hosting teacher—discussing and "naming" your practice with a peer challenges you to reflect on your instructional choices.

- For both teachers—discussing specific student behaviors during a class period can help both teachers think about their instruction and instructional choices.

Previsit Conference Guidelines

The purpose of the previsit conference is to review the teacher's lesson plan, including the goals, objectives, strategies/methodology, and assessment. If a face-to-face meeting is not possible, email communication is fine. Both the host teacher and the visiting teacher should complete their part of the previsit form and share with one another 24 hours prior to the visit.

Classroom Visit Guidelines

The visitor should arrive **at least 10 minutes before class**. (Ideally there is time for visiting and host teacher to talk before class, but if not, the visiting teacher should be there before class begins so as to be as unobtrusive in the visit as possible.)

The visitor can be briefly introduced to the students, with an equally brief explanation of why the visitor is present. The main purpose of the visit is to observe an action civics teacher in action, not to participate in the lesson. For that reason, it is best if the visitor not ask questions or participate in activities during class. The visitor should not have private conversations (with a student or another visitor) during class. The visitor and the host teacher should as much as possible reserve their communications until after the class is over.

There may be visits where the host teacher solicits participation of the visiting teacher. This participation is best if it is as an audience for their students to present to. Ideally the visiting teacher is not used as "another set of hands" in the classroom. While this can be a meaningful experience as well, it is not the purpose of these visits.

Consider Modes for Sharing Information Other Than Traditional Professional Development

Many people think of professional development as reading a book or watching someone speak. These have their place. But it's important to choose the mode that you expect will most likely get teachers in your building thinking about a complex approach like teaching and learning with social action. There are plenty of other ways to introduce new instructional strategies. In fact, it might seem better to call this "professional learning" rather than the traditional "professional development."

Discussing Articles and Videos on Teaching with Social Action

Here are a few examples of works that could generate interest as well as help teachers visualize how a project could unfold and what students would gain from it:

- **Student Research for Action.** This list of projects from What Kids Can Do helps educators see what's possible in social action projects. Good examples include "Deaf Students Teach Restaurants to Serve with Respect" and "Denver Teenagers Take Action for Social Change" (focused on a plan to build a new bridge that would destroy a local neighborhood). www .whatkidscando.org/specialcollections/student_research_action/index.html

- **"The Salad Girls: Students of PDS Alum Learn the Strength of Civic Action" (Savrock 2011).** This feature article from Penn State focuses on the role of the teachers featured in Chapter 1 of this book. www.ed.psu .edu/news/releases-jan-mar-2011/salad-girls

- *Meaningful Student Involvement: Guide to Students as Partners in School Change* **(Fletcher 2005).** This free, twenty-eight-page PDF from SoundOut.org focuses on change within schools. http://soundout.org /wp-content/uploads/2015/06/MSIGuide.pdf

- **"An Introduction to the Student Voice Movement: Student Voice Toolbox" (Fletcher).** This introduction from SoundOut.org describes essentials of the concept of student voice, including an explanation of how student voice differs from student engagement. http://soundout.org /category/tools/soundout-tools/articles/

- **Examples of Civic Action Projects.** This collection of six student videos from the Constitutional Rights Foundation shows students addressing a variety of issues. www.crfcap.org/mod/page/view.php?id=206

- **2013 Expeditionary Learning National Conference Keynote (Boyd et al. 2013).** In this thirty-two-minute video, Polaris Charter Academy students describe their anti-gun-violence campaign. http://vimeo.com/81395520

Articles and videos can be discussed in grade-level teams or subject-area department meetings or in mixed groups during professional development sessions.

Forming Teacher Study Groups or Professional Learning Communities (PLCs)

Much has been written about these, the most widely known proponents being Richard DuFour and his partners (see DuFour et al., *Learning by Doing: A Handbook for Professional Learning Communities at Work*, 2006). While some versions such as his focus heavily on data gathering and analysis, a broader approach is for teachers to study, collaborate on, and apply a larger strategy like social action projects. One thoughtful and up-to-date description of professional learning groups can be found in the Glossary of Education Reform (2014). It asserts, "Professional learning communities often function as a form of action research—i.e., as a way to continually question, reevaluate, refine, and improve teaching strategies and knowledge." A number of key characteristics are listed in the glossary:

- Groups meet regularly to work in agreed-upon ways to improve teaching and learning.

- They agree on common goals and expectations.

- They establish norms for how they work together, including ways to communicate respectfully and protocols for group discussion or problem solving.

- In many cases groups are facilitated by a trained group member.

Just as we know that students collaborate best when they are explicitly taught how to do so, groups of adults work together most effectively when they have agreed-upon procedures for their collaboration. A very extensive collection of protocols for guiding thoughtful and sensitive group discussions has been compiled by the National School Reform Faculty organization on its website at www.nsrfharmony.org/protocol/a_z.html. Some of the activities are more focused on team building, but several are especially valuable for group problem solving:

- The Charrette—an individual or team presents work in progress and gets feedback on a specific issue.

- Inquiry Circle—participants write in journals about times they were successful in their teaching and then share in pairs and in pairs of pairs.

- Critical Incident Protocol—an individual describes a problematic incident in class; the group then discusses it supportively while the presenter listens.

- Issaquah Protocol—a more complex version of the critical incident activity in which the group asks clarifying questions after the individual presents his or her problem. This is followed by more probing questions, and then the group discusses and considers suggestions while the presenter listens without participating.

It's fascinating to see how effective these activities can be at enabling a teacher who is struggling with a classroom problem to appreciate the input, rather than feeling criticized or put on the spot.

Share Data on Your Students' Success

At Reilly School (described in Chapter 6), the administration has been very supportive of the restorative justice program developed by art teacher Mauricio Pineda. However, Mauricio cautions that people always need reassurance that it's effective, and he repeatedly shares data on issues resolved by the peer council. As he says, "It's just like a fire—it always needs to be fed." As teachers and schools are flooded with more and more testing and data, however, let's not saddle ourselves with still more information that's arbitrary or disconnected from meaningful learning goals. The "Assessment" section in Chapter 5 provides guidelines for thoughtful and relevant assessment that helps students better connect with the audience(s) they are trying to reach. Don't hesitate to use the information to help convince others of the value of the projects you and your students have conducted. Teachers are not accustomed to bragging about successes, and don't like to alienate colleagues by claiming to be especially talented. But you need to show that learning with social action makes a difference for students.

So perhaps the way to approach this is to find respectful and egalitarian ways to share information. In one school, an instructional leadership team scheduled professional development sessions in which all teachers shared information on their successful practices. Teachers took turns circulating among tables that their colleagues manned in the cafeteria or gym. Everyone contributed, everyone learned, and no one was held up as a prized example.

Another consideration is timing. As you seek to widen the use of teaching with social action, when might be the best time to share your information? Data alone doesn't often convince people who are doubtful about a new idea. They will find counterarguments and ways to question its validity. But if your colleagues are already curious or interested and mainly need reassurance that they aren't taking a huge risk, and that kids will learn, then the data could be just the thing to help get them started.

Plan Your Campaign

So now it's time for the big picture. If you and your school (or department) are ready to develop a wider effort for teaching and learning with social action, it's time to map it out thoroughly and consider all the steps and angles. You can't anticipate everything, but it's a good idea to be intentional about your actions. (*Intentional* is frequently used organizer-speak for reminding people to think carefully about actions, rather than just dive in headfirst.) Here are some aspects of a campaign to think about.

Set Goals

It's good to be realistic about how much is possible at your school, but don't sell your-self short or start by aiming too low. People will respect you for being committed to something important, as long as you promote it in a respectful and constructive way and build supportive relationships. A series of step-by-step goals can help if you're con-cerned about moving too far too fast. SMART characteristics for goals were outlined in Chapter 3. Here they may be especially relevant. An effort should have goals that are specific, measurable, attainable, realistic, and timely.

It's wise, however, to aim for a larger goal like instituting social action projects rather than just a few narrow skills. And, when setting goals for student learning, you may want to include some of the mindsets that characterize active, responsible citizens, described in the discussion on assessment in Chapter 5:

> *Agency*—acting or exerting influence and power in a given situation
>
> *Belonging*—developing meaningful relationships with other students and adults and having a role in the classroom and at the school
>
> *Competence*—developing new abilities
>
> *Discourse*—exchanging diverse ideas and opinions to work toward a com-mon goal
>
> *Efficacy*—believing that one can make a difference in the world and that one has a responsibility to do so

All of these can be measured by observation, surveys, and testimony from other respon-sible adults—so they can indeed be SMART.

Consider the Possible Order for Various Steps in the Process

There's a lot to think about here. How and in what order will you build or strengthen connections with colleagues and the principal, and then bring up the idea of learning with social action across the school or department? One teacher who was seeking to promote a change at her school gathered signatures on a petition before talking with the principal. This backfired badly because he felt blindsided when she came to him with a seeming fait accompli.

So, take a moment to envision the entire process before you begin. Who are the stakeholders you'll need to reassure or at least respectfully listen to? What obstacles will you need to overcome (such as lack of time in the school's daily schedule)? What mode of informing teachers about the approach might work best in your setting? Once some teachers are trying it, how can you share information about efforts, successes, challenges? How can teachers help one another? What role can you encourage your administration to play (or *not* play)? What is a reasonable timeline for the overall effort?

As you're planning, try to find a "quick win" (a favorite of community organizers). This is what happened with the peace circles at Reilly School. When one student was the subject of much misinformed gossip, Mauricio Pineda set up a series of circles to reach all the students in that grade level, with the maligned student participating in each. Not only did the circumstances of the student's problem get clarified, but students stepped up to offer support to their beleaguered classmate. This outcome gave the strategy great credibility, and teachers began inviting Mauricio to their classrooms to try out circles as a regular classroom activity.

You've explored a number of key steps and strategies in this chapter. And it would be wonderful to be able to find answers to all your planning questions right here in this book. But they will all depend on the people and history and conditions in your school. The idea is to be intentional, to think about the various steps and options, and then make the most well-informed and considered decision that you can about each of them.

A Story of the Change Process at One School

At Alcott College Prep High School, Heather Van Benthuysen worked for several years on change in the school. She hoped to institute social action projects in many classrooms. But more broadly, she worked to help the building grow as a "Democracy School," where everyone has a voice and is active in the school community. The school had won an award from the McCormick Foundation, based primarily on the efforts of the after-school Social Justice League, which she organized with history teacher Jessica Marshall, who is now the head of Civic Engagement and Service Learning for Chicago Public Schools (for information on these awards in Illinois, visit www.mccormickfoundation.org/DemocracySchools2014). Some colleagues had viewed this as merely Heather's own pet project. To establish that the work was by and about the students, Heather encouraged the after-school Social Justice League to build a steady drumbeat of student-led activities. This created momentum over several years through the league's many initiatives (outlined in Chapter 7)—assemblies, discussions, visits to homerooms, posters, goals documents, celebrations.

Heather nurtured support from the principal by sending him regular emails and bringing him into Social Justice League meetings. She involved her English classes in the "Soap Box" speech competition on public issues sponsored by Chicago's Mikva

Challenge and convinced fellow department members to expand the competition to all freshman and AP English classes, all sophomore social studies classes, and some junior and senior courses. She promoted an annual spring "rhetorical throwdown" featuring storytelling, speeches, debates, and student films.

All this activity gradually stirred awareness among students, changing the tone of their thinking and their talk about the school. Teachers couldn't help but take notice. The assistant principal, Grace Moody, introduced a student leadership course. Another, Lucas Weisbecker, joined as a cosponsor of the Social Justice League. The principal put Heather in charge of professional development, but rather than just move ahead on her own, she submitted a year-long outline to the school's instructional leadership team. She started the year's professional development with a workshop on writing as a learning tool in all the subject areas, but first submitted that plan to the English department. She included a social studies and PE teacher in the session. The next professional development session linked writing to the larger democracy school theme, with other teachers taking more roles.

With a new dean for the school, the administration committed to the idea of "student voice" and constituted a "culture and climate" committee, making student involvement and activism a focus of the school. Having more of the faculty and administration on board was a major step, but presented new challenges. For example, the committee at first wanted to revise the "Civic Goals and Agreements" the league had drafted. Fortunately students were able to convince them to retain the original, to maintain its student ownership.

There's more of the story to unfold, not without its bumps. The development of a school where students have an active voice is a long process. Budget cuts and administrative changes make life in Chicago schools unpredictable. And the effort is now more than just Heather Van Benthuysen's or the league's. What we can do in this work is set students on a path, watch as they grow, and know that we're building future leaders for our communities. It's a path that other schools can take as well.

Take Care of Yourself

Campaigning for change like that taking place at Alcott College Prep can be demanding—and any teacher doing this kind of work must still, of course, stay focused on his or her own students every day as well. So it's essential to attend to your own well-being. There are basics not to be neglected—exercise, diet, friendship, family. All too many teachers' lounges and office warrens are stocked with junk food to help get through crises, hard to resist when the pressure is on.

Heather Van (as everyone calls her) has embarked on her own self-care plan. A first important step, she explains, is to tell the people in your life that you are doing this and want their support, since starting can be hard. As a result, for example, when her husband proposes weekend walks, she makes a point of agreeing, rather than clinging to her desk. Heather is now attending theater productions and pursuing her love of cooking by writing a cookbook with her sister. To tend to her health, she's committed to avoiding caffeine and sugar, drinking more water, and getting regular acupuncture.

She's encouraging herself to assume that people act with the best intentions. While she pushes her students and holds high expectations for them, she looks for more opportunities to celebrate with them. Feeling positive and avoiding a deficit view of conditions and people in her job is actually a part of taking care of herself, she believes, saying, "We can only move in the direction we imagine."

This description of Heather's detailed self-care is offered to emphasize that taking care of oneself is not simply a matter of getting more sleep each night: it's a plan that's every bit as strategic as your work with students each day. Even if your list is not as expansive as Heather's, you can seek out spaces in your life to lighten and broaden your own experiences. Though this takes time, it gives you necessary fresh energy for the work in return.

WRAPPING UP

This book has been written to help teachers guide and support a kind of learning that enables students to act as responsible citizens in their communities—by empowering them to be active and responsible citizens *now*. The success of this approach has been confirmed over and over by the stories and examples in this book, and the many more across our country that may not be chronicled here but that take place day by day. Kids of all ages are capable of far more than we generally expect, and this work helps them to discover that they have a voice, often a voice they didn't know they had, a voice that adults take seriously. And in the process of this work, students learn a wide range of skills—the very skills that more rigidly structured standards are actually supposed to promote. Kids gain much essential knowledge about how to research an issue, work together, make thoughtful plans, communicate smartly, and take a productive role in a democratic community. They learn about their strengths and the ways they need to grow. And they learn that, rather than becoming cynical about social problems and flawed public institutions, they can take strategic action to improve them.

This learning and experience is needed throughout our country to help make it the equitable, open, and democratic place we want it to be. Each teacher who carries out this kind of teaching and learning moves us in that direction. That is how community and democracy get built: one classroom at a time, with the students you have right now. There are obstacles, and each of us is just one person. But it's joyful, energizing work, and our students know it is powerful when they experience it. That's what will keep it growing.

RESOURCES

Core Thinking and Research on Teaching and Learning with Social Action

Carnegie Corp. of New York and the Center for Information and Research on Civic Learning and Engagement. 2003. *The Civic Mission of Schools.* http://civicmission .s3.amazonaws.com/118/f7/1/172/2003_Civic_Mission_of_Schools_Report.pdf.

Dover, Alison. 2009. "Teaching for Social Justice and K–12 Student Outcomes: A Conceptual Framework and Research Review." *Equity & Excellence in Education* 42 (4): 507–525.

Fletcher, Adam. "An Introduction to the Student Voice Movement." SoundOut.org. http://soundout.org/category/tools/soundout-tools/articles/.

Fletcher, Adam. 2005. *Meaningful Student Involvement: Guide to Students as Partners in School Change.* 2nd edition. Soundout.org. http://soundout.org/wp-content /uploads/2015/06/MSIGuide.pdf.

Kahne, Joseph, and Susan Sporte. 2007. "Developing Citizens: The Impact of Civic Learning Opportunities on Students' Commitment to Civic Participation." *American Educational Research Journal* 45 (3): 738–766.

Kirshner, Ben. 2015. *Youth Activism in an Era of Education Inequality.* New York: New York University Press. Outstanding qualitative research on student activism.

Levinson, Meira. 2012. *No Citizen Left Behind.* Cambridge MA: Harvard University Press. Essential philosophical underpinnings of learning with social action.

Mitra, Dana, and Stephanie Serriere. 2012. "Student Voice in Elementary School Reform: Examining Youth Development in Fifth Graders." *American Educational Research Journal* 49 (4): 743–774.

Robbins, Elizabeth. 2013. "Young People Are the Now." Talk at TEDxWellsStreetED . www.youtube.com/watch?v=7-lUrM-rmIE.

Accounts of Civic Action Projects (with Some Help on Implementation)

Assaf, Lori Czop, and Joel Johnson. 2014. "A Call for Action: Engaging in Purposeful Real-World Writing." *Voices from the Middle* 21 (3): 24–33.

Berdan, Kristina, et al., eds. 2006. *Writing for a Change: Boosting Literacy and Learning Through Social Action.* San Francisco: Jossey-Bass and Berkeley, CA: National Writing Project. See especially her Chapter 5, "Reflections on the Youth Dreamers."

Berdan, Kristina, et al. 2014. *I Am Not a Test Score: Lessons Learned from Dreaming.* Baltimore, MD: Youth Dreamers Foundation.

Boyd, Kameron, Desiree Gabarin, De'Angelo Pinkston, and Ameera Rollins. 2013. Keynote address by Polaris Academy students, 2013 Expeditionary Learning National Conference. https://vimeo.com/81395520.

Children First Network 102. 2011. *Student-Led School Improvement: Work, Findings, and Next Steps.* New York: New York City Dept. of Education.

Constitutional Rights Foundation. "Civic Action Project—Student Action." www .crfcap.org/mod/page/view.php?id=206.

Generation Citizen. "Generation Citizen Stories." www.generationcitizen.org/stories /list/. Examples of student projects.

Harris, Mildred, et al. 2006. "The Story of the Youth Dreamers: In Their Own Words." In *Writing for a Change: Boosting Literacy and Learning Through Social Action*, edited by Kristina Berdan et al. San Francisco: Jossey-Bass.

Kaulessar, Ricardo. 2015. "Montclair Kimberley Students Write Letters for Social Change." *NorthJersey.com.* July 7. www.northjersey.com/news/education/letters-to -make-the-world-better-1.1369881?page=all.

Laub, Paula. 2006. "Power Play." In *Writing for a Change: Boosting Literacy and Learning Through Social Action,* edited by Kristina Berdan et al. San Francisco: Jossey-Bass.

Mills, Heidi, et al. 2014. "Changing Hearts, Minds, and Actions Through Collaborative Inquiry." *Language Arts* 92 (1): 36–51.

Oyler, Celia. 2012. *Actions Speak Louder Than Words: Community Activism as Curriculum.* New York: Routledge.

Savrock, Joe. 2011. "The Salad Girls: Students of PDS Alum Learn the Strength of Civic Action." Penn State College of Education News. www.ed.psu.edu/news/releases -jan-mar-2011/salad-girls.

Schultz, Brian. 2008. *Spectacular Things Happen Along the Way: Lessons from an Urban Classroom.* New York: Teachers College Press.

Serriere, Stephanie, Dana Mitra, and Jennifer Cody. 2010. "Young Citizens Take Action for Better School Lunches." *Social Studies and the Young Learner* 23 (2): 4–8.

What Kids Can Do. "Student Research for Action." www.whatkidscando.org/special-collections/student_research_action/index.html. Thirteen examples of student projects, including "Deaf Students Teach Restaurants to Serve with Respect" and Denver teenagers action on a plan for a new bridge that would destroy a local neighborhood.

Guiding Civic Action Projects

Bomer, Randy, and Katherine Bomer. 2001. *For a Better World: Reading and Writing for Social Action.* Portsmouth, NH: Heinemann.

Clements, Andrew, and Elivia Savadier. 1992. *Billy and the Bad Teacher.* Saxonville, MA: Picture Book Studio.

Daniels, Harvey, and Sara Ahmed. 2015. *Upstanders: How to Engage Middle School Hearts and Minds with Inquiry.* Portsmouth, NH: Heinemann.

Earth Force. 2004. *Community Action Problem Solving Teacher Guide.* Curriculum. Paper 36. http://digitalcommons.unomaha.edu/slcecurriculum/36

Fletcher, Adam. 2014. *The Practice of Youth Engagement.* CreateSpace Independent Publishing Platform.

Generation Citizen. http://generationcitizen.org/. Programs in four U.S. locations support students' civic action projects.

Institute for Community Research, Youth Action Research Institute. *Participatory Action Research Curriculum for Empowering Youth.* www.incommunityresearch.org/research/yari.htm.

Mikva Challenge. 2015. *Issues to Action Curriculum.* www.mikvachallenge.org. Outstanding detailed curriculum guide.

Millenson, Daniel, Molly Mills, and Sarah Andes. 2014. *Making Civics Relevant, Making Citizens Effective: Action Civics in the Classroom.* New York: IDEBATE Press.

National Action Civics Collaborative. "Action Civics Toolbox." http://actioncivics collaborative.org/resources/toolbox/.

National Youth Leadership Council. www.nylc.org. The largest organization focused on service learning. Its standards stress student voice and leadership, in-depth research on issues, and robust action in the community.

Project Citizen. www.civiced.org/programs/project-citizen. Professional development in most states, plus online courses and textbooks.

"Student Voice Research and Practice." Facebook page. www.facebook.com/groups/studentvoicepage/. Teachers share info on student voice in schools and communities.

Wilhelm, Jeffrey, Whitney Douglas, and Sara Fry. 2014. *The Activist Learner: Inquiry, Literacy, and Service to Make Learning Matter.* New York: Teachers College Press and Berkeley, CA: National Writing Project.

Youth On Board. *15 Points: Successfully Involving Young People* and related publications. www.youthonboard.org/. Sponsors the Boston Student Advisory Council and provides training and consultation in schools around the country.

Additional Tools and Information for Action Civics Projects

Byrne, Richard. 2010. "Free Guide—Making Videos on the Web." www.freetech4teachers .com/2010/05/free-guide-making-videos-on-web.html.

Chase, Brett. 2014. "Cracking the Code on School Lunches at CPS." BGA. Dec. 14. www .bettergov.org/cracking_the_code_on_school_lunches_at_cps/?KeywordId=23.

K–12 Tech Tools. "Cameras and Video Tools." http://edutechdatabase.wikispaces.com /Cameras+%26+Video+Tools.

PBS *American High* Teachers Lounge. "Lesson 1: Creating Great Audio for Video." www.pbs.org/americanhigh/teachers/lesson1.html.

Soechtig, Stephanie. 2014. "Fed Up" (film). http://fedupmovie.com/#/page/home.

Building Classroom Climate

Bixler, Betty. "Learning Style Inventory." www.personal.psu.edu/bxb11/LSI/LSI.htm.

Daniels, Harvey, and Nancy Steineke. 2014. *Teaching the Social Skills of Academic Interaction.* Thousand Oaks, CA: Corwin.

Edutopia. "Multiple Intelligences Self-Assessment." www.edutopia.org/multiple -intelligences-assessment.

Farrington, Camille, et al. 2012. *Teaching Adolescents to Become Learners: The Role of Noncognitive Factors in Shaping School Performance: A Critical Literature Review.* University of Chicago Consortium on Chicago School Research. http://ccsr .uchicago.edu/sites/default/files/publications/Noncognitive%20Report.pdf.

Freedom Writers Foundation. "Line Game." www.freedomwritersfoundation.org /lesson-plans/lesson-1.

Learning-Styles-Online.com. "Discover Your Learning Styles—Graphically!" http:// learning-styles-online.com.

McCloud, Carol, and David Messing. 2006. *Have You Filled a Bucket Today? A Guide to Daily Happiness for Kids.* Northville, MI: Ferne Press.

Steineke, Nancy. 2002. *Reading and Writing Together: Collaborative Literacy in Action.* Portsmouth, NH: Heinemann.

Supporting Students' Research

Aye, Sarah Cantor. "Designing Everything but the Food." Video talk. Greater Good Studio. www.greatergoodstudio.com/videos/.

Brooks, Sarah. 2011. "Design for Social Innovation: An Interview with Ezio Manzini." Shareable.net. July 26. www.shareable.net/blog/design-for-social-innovation-an -interview-with-ezio-manzini.

Center for Information and Research on Civic Learning and Engagement. www.civic youth.org/tools-for-practice/youth-led-research-resource-page/. See especially their examples of youth-led research.

Cooperrider, D. L., and D. Whitney. 2001. "A Positive Revolution in Change." In *Appreciative Inquiry: An Emerging Direction for Organization Development,* edited by D. L. Cooperrider et al., 9–29. Champaign, IL: Stipes.

Couric, Katie. "Katie Couric on How to Conduct a Good Interview." https://www.youtube.com/watch?v=4eOynrI2eTM.

Dreamtown Realty. Dreamtown—The Chicago Neighborhoods Guide. www.dreamtown.com/neighborhoods/chicago-neighborhoods.html. Example of a community information resource.

Greater Good Studio. "New Frontiers Innovation Lab." PowerPoint presentation (2013) in Chicago.

Harvey, Stephanie, and Harvey Daniels. 2015. *Comprehension and Collaboration: Inquiry Circles in Action.* Portsmouth, NH: Heinemann.

Positive Deviance Initiative. 2014. "Spotlight Case Study: Vietnam as a Prototype for the PD Approach." www.positivedeviance.org/about_pd/case_studies.html.

Sternin, Jerry. 2009. "The Vietnam Story." www.positivedeviance.org/about_pd/Monique%20VIET%20NAM%20CHAPTER%20Oct%2017.pdf. *Positive deviance* is another, rather technical-sounding term for appreciative inquiry.

What Kids Can Do. "Sample Student, Teacher, and School-Specific Surveys." www.whatkidscando.org/specialcollections/student_as_allies/pdfs/saa_samplesurveys_final.pdf.

Assessment, Standards, and Tests

Allensworth, Elaine, et al. 2008. *From High School to the Future: ACT Preparation—Too Much, Too Late.* Chicago: Chicago Consortium on School Research.

National Action Civics Collaborative. "Standard Action Civics Student Post-Survey." http://actioncivicscollaborative.org/resources/toolbox/.

Implementing Classroom Workshop

Atwell, Nancie. 1998. *In the Middle: New Understandings About Writing, Reading, and Learning.* Portsmouth, NH: Heinemann.

Calkins, Lucy. 2013, 2014. *Units of Study in Opinion, Information, and Narrative Writing.* Portsmouth, NH: Heinemann. Series with guidebook sets for each grade level, K–8.

Daniels, Harvey, Steven Zemelman, and Nancy Steineke. 2007. *Content-Area Writing: Every Teacher's Guide.* Portsmouth, NH: Heinemann.

Fletcher, Ralph, and JoAnn Portalupi. 2001. *Writing Workshop: The Essential Guide.* Portsmouth, NH: Heinemann.

Graves, Donald. 1983. *Writing: Teachers and Children at Work.* Portsmouth, NH: Heinemann.

Introducing Restorative Justice

Alternatives, Inc. "Restorative Peer Juries."

Cohen, Richard. "Quick Guide to Implementing a Peer Mediation Program." School Mediation Associates. www.schoolmediation.com/pdf/Quick-Guide-to -Implementing-a-Peer-Mediation-Program.pdf.

Cohen, Richard. 2005. *Students Resolving Conflict: Peer Mediation in Schools.* 2nd edition. Culver City, CA: Good Year Books.

Engaging Schools. "Resolving Conflict Creatively Program." http://engagingschools.org /?s=Resolving+Conflict+Creatively+Program.

Fix School Discipline. 2015. "Educator Toolkit." http://fixschooldiscipline.org /educator-toolkit/. Focused on California, with examples from California schools, but relevant elsewhere.

Illinois Criminal Justice Information Authority. *Implementing Restorative Justice: A Guide for Schools.* www.icjia.state.il.us/public/pdf/BARJ/SCHOOL%20BARJ %20GUIDEBOOOK.pdf.

International Institute for Restorative Practices. 2014. *Improving School Climate: Evidence from Schools Implementing Restorative Practices.* www.iirp.edu/pdf /ImprovingSchoolClimate.pdf.

Klasovsky, Jean. 2013. "Repairing Our Schools Through Restorative Justice." Talk at TEDxWellsStreetED. https://www.youtube.com/watch?v=tqktOiYG5NM.

Klasovsky, Jean, et al. 2010. "Restorative Practices Handbook." Self-published.

Losen, Daniel, et al. 2015. *Are We Closing the School Discipline Gap?* Los Angeles: Center for Civil Rights, University of California at Los Angeles.

Mikaelsen, Ben. 2002. *Touching Spirit Bear.* New York: HarperCollins.

Mirsky, Laura. 2004. "Restorative Justice Practices of Native American, First Nation and Other Indigenous People of North America." *Restorative Practices Forum.* April 27. International Institute for Restorative Practices. www.iirp.edu/iirpWebsites/web /uploads/article_pdfs/natjust1.pdf.

Mirsky, Laura, and Steve Korr. 2014. "Restoring Community and Trust." *Principal Leadership.* February 2014.

Peace Education Foundation. www.peaceeducation.org/index.html.

Pranis, Kay, and Barry Stuart. 2000. "Establishing Shared Responsibility for Child Welfare Through Peacemaking Circles." In *Family Group Conferencing*, edited by Gail Buford and Joe Hudson. New Brunswick, N.J.: Aldine Transaction. Available in adapted form at Project Nia website, www.project-nia.org/docs/Peacemaking _Circles_overview.pdf.

Pranis, Kay. 2005. *The Little Book of Circle Processes: A New/Old Approach to Peacemaking.* New York: Good Books.

Pranis, Kay, and Carolyn Boyes-Watson. 2015. *Circle Forward: Building a Restorative School Community.* St. Paul, MN: Living Justice Press.

Restorative Practices Working Group. 2014. *Restorative Practices: Fostering Healthy Relationships and Promoting Positive Discipline in Schools.* Advancement Project, AFT, NEA, and National Opportunity to Learn Campaign. http://b.3cdn.net/advancement/5d8bec1cdf51cb38ec_60m6y18hu.pdf.

Robert R. McCormick Foundation. "Illinois Democracy Schools." www.mccormick foundation.org/DemocracySchools2014.

Study Guides and Strategies. Cooperative Learning Series. "Peer Mediation." www .studygs.net/peermed.htm.

Wachtel, Ted. 2013. "Defining Restorative." International Institute for Restorative Practices Graduate School. www.iirp.edu/pdf/Defining-Restorative.pdf.

Promoting Change in Schools

DuFour, Richard, et al. 2006. *Learning by Doing: A Handbook for Professional Learning Communities at Work.* Bloomington, IN: Solution Tree.

Fullan, Michael, and Andy Hargreaves. 1996. *What's Worth Fighting for in Your School.* New York: Teachers College Press.

Glossary of Education Reform. 2014. "Professional Learning Community." http:// edglossary.org/professional-learning-community/. A thoughtful discussion of this strategy

Hargreaves, Andy, and Dean Fink. 2006. *Sustainable Leadership.* San Francisco: Jossey-Bass.

Lambert, Linda. 1998. *Building Leadership Capacity in Schools.* Alexandria, VA: Association for Supervision and Curriculum Development.

McDonald, Joseph, et al. 2007. *The Power of Protocols: An Educator's Guide to Better Practice.* 2nd edition. New York: Teachers College Press.

National School Reform Faculty. "NSRF Protocols and Activities . . . from A to Z." www.nsrfharmony.org/free-resources/protocols/a-z.

Zemelman, Steven, and Harry Ross. 2009. *13 Steps to Teacher Empowerment: Taking a More Active Role in Your School Community.* Portsmouth, NH: Heinemann.

INDEX